Redesigning Special Education Systems through Collaborative Problem Solving

Special education is facing a period of increasing conflict, which is leading to untenable jobs and an exodus from the field. This important and innovative book offers a framework that can begin to resolve many of the consequential challenges special educators, schools and students are dealing with.

Through a framing of effective leadership built through authentic collaboration, this book outlines how we might stop viewing the issues in special education as insurmountable problems and instead see them as informative starting points from which to communicate, brainstorm and organize operative partnerships to find solutions, change practices and create better outcomes at the level of entire districts, as well as individual schools.

Redesigning Special Education Systems Through Collaborative Problem Solving is key reading for school and district leaders and administrators, special education teachers and preservice teachers interested in becoming more productively engaged in creating solutions and making changes in the field of special education.

Michelle Brenner is the Executive Director of Special Education for Boulder Valley School District in Boulder, Colorado. As a special educator since 2005, she has worked in three different states and is dedicated to inclusive and collaborative innovations in special education practices that improve student outcomes to build a more inclusive society.

Kelly Miller is a Board Certified Behavior Analyst, Licensed Clinical Social Worker and Autism Consultant for Boulder Valley Schools since 2005. She has assisted her district in leading the state's inclusive autism practices with a focus on multidisciplinary approaches to assessment, goal writing and service delivery.

Also Available from Routledge Eye On Education

Successfully Launching into Young Adulthood with ADHD: Firsthand Guidance for Parents and Educators Supporting Children with Neurodevelopmental Differences
Chris A. Zeigler Dendy and Ruth Hughes

The Self-Determined Learning Model of Instruction: A Practitioner's Guide to Implementation for Special Education
Karrie A. Shogren and Sheida K. Raley

Supporting Your Child with Special Needs: 50 Fundamental Tools for Families
Rachel R. Jorgensen

Loving Your Job in Special Education: 50 Tips and Tools
Rachel R. Jorgensen

Redesigning Special Education Systems through Collaborative Problem Solving
A Guidebook for School Leaders

Michelle Brenner and Kelly Miller

NEW YORK AND LONDON

Designed Cover Image: Cover by Cole Brenner at BRENNERds.com.

First published 2024
by Routledge
605 Third Avenue, New York, NY 10158

and by Routledge
4 Park Square, Milton Park, Abingdon, Oxon, OX14 4RN

Routledge is an imprint of the Taylor & Francis Group, an informa business

© 2024 Michelle Brenner and Kelly Miller

The right of Michelle Brenner and Kelly Miller to be identified as authors of this work has been asserted in accordance with sections 77 and 78 of the Copyright, Designs and Patents Act 1988.

All rights reserved. No part of this book may be reprinted or reproduced or utilised in any form or by any electronic, mechanical, or other means, now known or hereafter invented, including photocopying and recording, or in any information storage or retrieval system, without permission in writing from the publishers.

Trademark notice: Product or corporate names may be trademarks or registered trademarks, and are used only for identification and explanation without intent to infringe.

Library of Congress Cataloging-in-Publication Data
Names: Brenner, Michelle (Special educator), author. | Miller, Kelly (Autism consultant), author.
Title: Redesigning special education systems through collaborative problem solving : a guidebook for school leaders / Michelle Brenner and Kelly Miller.
Description: First edition. | New York : Routledge, 2024. | Includes bibliographical references.
Identifiers: LCCN 2023047512 (print) | LCCN 2023047513 (ebook) | ISBN 9781032592534 (hbk) | ISBN 9781032589947 (pbk) | ISBN 9781003453826 (ebk)
Subjects: LCSH: Special education--Research.
Classification: LCC LC3965 .B74 2024 (print) | LCC LC3965 (ebook) | DDC 371.9072--dc23/eng/20231129
LC record available at https://lccn.loc.gov/2023047512
LC ebook record available at https://lccn.loc.gov/2023047513

ISBN: 978-1-032-59253-4 (hbk)
ISBN: 978-1-032-58994-7 (pbk)
ISBN: 978-1-003-45382-6 (ebk)

DOI: 10.4324/9781003453826

Typeset in Palatino
by SPi Technologies India Pvt Ltd (Straive)

Contents

1. Introduction: Why Do We Need to Redesign Special Education? 1
2. The Power Is in the Process 14
3. Six Not-So-Easy Steps for Collaborative Change........31
4. Leveraging Unexpected Partnerships..................47
5. Modeling Collaboration: A Parallel Adult Learning Process....................................62
6. Empowering Others 76
7. Strength of Students...............................91
8. Attracting and Retaining Quality Staff 106
9. Designing Your Innovation 122

1

Introduction

Why Do We Need to Redesign Special Education?

When someone says "special education," there are a vast array of visceral reactions that one might observe. Sometimes we see the compassionate response with an empathetic brow lift by those who think special education is the service-oriented, world-changing, do-gooder work that everyone should aspire to. If you're talking to a parent of a student with special needs, you might get a hug and a smile as they recollect the many individuals who have cared for and changed the lives of their own children. Meanwhile, other parents of students with disabilities respond with a physical retreat as they recall the fight they had in order to get their own child what they wanted from the system, or they recall the restraints, phone calls home, tears and concerns that this system brings up for them. If you're talking with a school administrator, you might see an inquisitive look as they recall all the best hopes of their special education teams but simultaneously the barriers and challenges to realizing what they want to achieve for their students.

Special education is a system designed for equity to help students with disabilities achieve access to, and progress in, their educational systems. The rules and regulations that have been labeled "special education" have created a system that provides "more than 7.5 million children with disabilities with special education and related services" ("A History of the Individuals," 2023). On the surface, this is really incredible work in shifting our country from excluding "1.8 million children with disabilities from public schools" to an inclusive educational system where all students are educated. From 1975 until 2020, there has been overwhelming progress through the various regulations, most recently the reauthorization of the Individuals with Disabilities Education Act (IDEA).[1] The IDEA regulations have made free appropriate public education (FAPE) available to children who are eligible under its criteria. Each year, an eligible student must have an updated Individualized Education Program (IEP) that is created to define their needs, services, accommodations and placement to receive their FAPE. The concept of the IEP as the collaborative cornerstone of the IDEA regulation has innovated and protected this progress on behalf of our students in the United States.

And yet, the best of intentions has left educators and families fraught with challenges in the practical applications of IDEA. While the theoretical intention is for a team to sit down and problem-solve a collective plan on behalf of a student with a disability, IEP meetings have become more of a boxing ring of taking sides. Similar to boxing, IEP meetings have become a process with a ringside judge, participants taking corners with their own coaches or advocates and a system of winners or losers. We even send out invitations to attend the main event. Educators and parents alike could understand the feeling of being "on the ropes" at an IEP meeting as we pin each other with questions and requests that we are not prepared for.

The ever-evolving and dynamic special education system has led to laws being tested and challenged and educational leaders always trying to manage a system where funding is not enough to meet the needs that these laws expect of the system. We are led to make decisions about the most basic needs and resources of our students rather than open availability to make decisions without thinking of related implications. The promise of IDEA has never been realized in terms of funding, and yet we have to make decisions about services without considering the cost. Any special education leader will smirk at that little fun fact. Go ahead and try to spend $100,000 more than you are budgeted because a new student moves in and needs something you didn't plan for. We all have our ways to figure it out, but that is the definition of being between a rock and a hard place.

> Only in the past few years has Washington's share of special education funding risen higher than about 12 percent, despite Congress' 1975 promise to pay 40 percent of the incremental costs of educating students with disabilities pursuant to federal mandates. Meanwhile, those mandates—elaborated by Congress, the Education Department, and the federal courts—have steadily raised the financial obligations of states and school districts, and the number of students receiving special education services has soared.
>
> (Finn et al., 2001)

When schools shut down in March 2020 for the COVID-19 pandemic, what was challenging before became an impossible scenario for most leaders of special education. Parents often say that this time sent their children with disabilities into a tailspin. Educators recall that we had to reinvent how we teach almost overnight. Parents and educators alike have not felt the rebound of this period in time, and most of us recognize that the landscape of special education is now very different as a result. This book is intended to help our fellow school-based and district-based leaders of special education to find some positive pathways through the current impossible state of special education in our systems.

We are going to let you in on a little secret. School-based leaders often want the same things that parents want for students. We join the educational system full of inspiration and belief that we can make a difference. We do the work to make things better and to see the successes of our students. Nothing makes us happier than creating systems and plans that work and to see exponential growth for students. When we watch our students with disabilities grow through our system and gain the skills to read, write, do math, hold a job, go to college and live a successful life that they desire, special education leaders are filled with pride. We tell our families stories about "our kids" and hang photos on our walls, caring for students as we would our own families. We want what parents and students want. As special education leaders, we also understand that we are not in a candy shop with infinite resources and choices available to us. We work within a system of rules that say educational services are within this box and boundary, funding is in this boundary, time has limits and there are limits in staff available to hire. We are always weighing wants and needs. We are constantly battling with our vision to change the system while working within the parameters of the system we are in. The arrangement of resources in special education is much more easily compared to a task of extreme couponing rather than a shopping spree.

In *Rethinking Special Education for a New Century*, one author wrote of this battle as,

> a legal and policy straitjacket, creating a system that is full of adversarial procedures, rife with litigation, unresponsive to innovation, discouraging to diversity and hostile to creativity.
>
> (Finn et al., 2001)

In recent years, parents have observed their children's education in more depth due to the school closures and virtual learning that happened during the pandemic. The culture of education has shifted where teachers/educators are frequently devalued, and communities feel empowered to question the expertise of trained staff. This could be in part because of these COVID closures, where parents realized that there is not any magic in the work of teachers. Education is, in fact, hard work and filled with overwhelming requirements where there is never a quick fix. What sometimes looks like magical outcomes is the result of years of training, merging various efforts and resources together and significant work alongside students over long periods of time. Being highly skilled at teaching doesn't look like being a pro-athlete where you can clearly see that this person has a talent that you could never achieve. The reality is that skilled teachers masterfully balance so many things to ensure students make progress, but when done well, it looks easy and reproducible. How many of us can implement a 45-minute group with 5 students where we plan to teach how to blend digraphs together to read sentences while managing Suzanne's behavior intervention plan, managing Joey's attention breaks and need for fidgets to be switched every 5 minutes, respond to the office phone call that a parent is waiting for a meeting, gather progress data on the progress chart, prompt a student's social goals for reciprocal conversation and address the student who was just sent to you for not sitting and behaving in class? All of this is happening at the same time while requiring evidence of student growth and progress. I recently had a parent scoff at the idea that a teacher was doing three to four things simultaneously for the intended outcome for their child. They thought it was impossible and didn't believe the information we were sharing. Not only is this true, but it is also what happens all day long for our teachers.

We are also noticing a shift in expectations. Suddenly, having students with disabilities in schools who are making progress, once big wins from IDEA regulation, doesn't feel like enough anymore. Parents and communities want more. Special education leaders also want more. We are moving from a system where being in a school and making progress is the goal to a national movement where we expect greater postsecondary outcomes for our students and gap-closing student results at lightning speed. With expectations being raised and the state and national systems not keeping up with those expectations, we end up in constant conflict while we are working at an unreasonable pace to just keep up.

If you do a Google search for recent challenges in special education, you'll get hundreds of links defining just some of the recent issues. A few notable challenges include the following:

- Soaring mental health needs
- Deepening shortage of qualified teachers
- Burnout and retention of existing special education staff
- Increasing paperwork

- Increased costs and decreased funding
- Disproportionate identification of students on IEPs
- Lack of systems for training general education staff
- Increasing aggressive behavior in inclusive schools
- Decreased specialized or separate school availability
- Increased time on paperwork and compliance and long IEP meetings
- Increase use of dispute resolution and legal processes

Take a pause here and add to this list. What additional challenges are impacting your work to lead special education currently? If you are reading this book, we are certain you can list a few more.

- _____
- _____
- _____
- _____
- _____
- _____

When I started out in special education leadership, I recall that if a parent asked to change a goal or questioned more services, it was a unique and dynamic meeting. My work was much more focused on leading the mindsets and beliefs around inclusive practices, differentiation, co-teaching and developing understanding of disability and disability rights. There wasn't as much time spent in contentious and long IEP meetings, and we didn't have much dispute resolution. I was able to help my teachers focus on the skill of teaching. Now I am asked frequently to host professional development around how to manage IEP meetings that last over three hours or strategies to work with advocates. I'm asked to have our lawyer provide annual updates rather than share best practices in teaching autistic students. I often need to reserve calendar time to help teachers through deep anxiety about emails they are receiving from families. As hard as we try to work through this new pattern of requests, this often results in educators resigning or taking leaves of absence to manage the chronic stress of the special education role.

We hear from teachers right now that they can earn more waiting tables than working as special education teachers. I did an exit interview with a teacher this year, and he described that he was criticized for coming in late or not meeting paperwork deadlines. He explained how his principal wouldn't listen to him, that he had to get home to his kids quickly when the bell rang and then he would work in the evenings to catch up. His wife had left him, and he needed to get his kids to school, but the drop-off lines often made him ten minutes late. He promised that he was never late enough to miss picking up students from the bus to start their day. He had given up his plan time almost daily due to paraeducators/aides who were calling out sick and then a lack of subs filling the jobs. He was still paying college loans and loved teaching the students; however, he could not continue the stress of being questioned on a daily basis about schedules, paperwork and what was observed on the surface. The leadership system for him was based in compliance and attendance, but not in looking at the whole scope of what was asked of him. No one thought to provide collaborative solutions. Additionally, the parents of his students more and more expected emails and phone calls all day and night and on the weekends, and he just couldn't meet their expectations and care for his own children as a single dad. By the time we spoke and discussed if he might want another school location or a different position for a fresh start, he was burnt out. He said he could have a more consistent schedule at a local restaurant and make almost as much money. He needed to make this change for his own mental health and to be a better father to his children.

A few months later, I received an email from a parent who was fighting to move their child from this same school where the teacher left midyear. The parent had hired an advocate and insisted that their child's need for consistency was impacted by the teacher leaving. They quoted IDEA regulations and shared their position that we needed to make an individualized decision to move the child's school to ensure consistency, which they argued was critically important to that child's progress. Of course, I couldn't tell the parents all the reasons for this teacher leaving the profession. I couldn't tell them that the next closest school had a teacher who was way over caseload and was at risk of leaving if they had another student placed with them. I couldn't tell them that we were simultaneously panicking about hiring four other special education teachers at that very moment due to the hiring shortage. They wouldn't understand that the sub shortage was impacting everyone and that the next schools were not going to provide anything different or more consistent for their child. What I really wanted them to do was to have the student stay at the current school, a place where their child would have the most consistency possible, a place where we could all compassionately care for the new teacher and paraeducators who were showing up in August with the excitement to care for this student, having already read the IEP and begun building boxes of individual materials for them. If they helped us support this new teacher, and if I helped the principal set up a new culture of caring and partnership, then we could limit the turnover in this classroom. But how can we resolve this challenge with a family who is spending hundreds of dollars on an advocate whose only goal is to find a new school? I won't yet share how we solved this challenge, but I'd ask you to think about how you might use our theme of redesigning with collaboration if this were your scenario.

All of these challenges and this historical background have left us in our current reality right now as special education leaders. We can't change where we are; however, we can find new and innovative ways to lead in this modern environment.

This book is in no way criticizing the parents, advocates, emails and needs that precipitated this change. You'll see the theme throughout this book that special education leaders need the advocacy and pressures from the community and parents to help identify needs and make changes together. We want to meet with our community, advocates and parents and understand the themes that they are seeing so we can address them and reduce conflicts. We absolutely know we are better together.

It comes as no surprise to anyone who knows about special education that we need to lead this work differently than we have done before. We need to redesign special education in how we work together in both our advocacy and our collaboration to create the visionary outcomes we all desire for our students. The changes we are seeing are indicators that the federal IEP process and IDEA rules are not enough to make the changes needed. As leaders, we have to do something more and different to address our current situation. By changing our approach from compliance and managing the process to a collaborative and system-wide partnership, we believe we can redesign how we work on behalf of our students and begin to resolve many of our current challenges.

What if we saw all of these challenges as communications rather than problems? Our ever-growing staffing shortage isn't a crisis; let's say it is a communication from our system. That might lead us to look at the work as a message or symptom that we need to listen to rather than a challenge or barrier. What if we looked at increased paperwork as a communication rather than a barrier? What does increased paperwork tell us about the system? Might it tell us that our parents need more communication than a once-a-year IEP meeting? Might it tell us that our progress monitoring systems are not efficient enough to easily embed into our progress reports and IEPs? Maybe we would learn that that input process itself is cumbersome and could be improved. What if we looked at increasing behaviors in our schools as a communication rather than a barrier? What could this tell us about the system? Might we need to consider additional training or structures to support those students? Maybe use resources in a different way for prevention or possibly partner with community groups who are working through the same changes to design something together. If we redesigned *how* we think about the challenges in special education to instead see these as communications that inform us about the work that needs to be done, could we solve things in a different way?

Take a moment and look at the challenges you added to the list a few pages back. Reflect on what those challenges might be telling us if we view them as communications.

> **BOX 1.1   Reflection**

The authors of this book in no way believe we have the answers all figured out. We see the current landscape and can offer some of the strategies that have worked for us over the last 20 years to help others find new energy and solutions to lead this work. Collectively, we have been educational leaders for over 35 years. We've seen a lot of things that don't work. We have that same world-changing vision for the work mentioned earlier in the chapter, and that inspires us to help others make changes. We see so many teachers and administrators and special education leaders leave the field because they can't make the impact they want. We have observed in our district, our state (Colorado), at national conferences and through international consulting that special education has so much power to change our world. However, if we keep doing things the way we have always done them, we will keep getting the same results.

We also have this worry that people we work with will read this book and call out the many times we haven't been collaborative or the many times that they don't get what they want from our work and our systems. We don't always get things right in our work. We both make mistakes every day. We also know that this is very hard work that takes constant daily effort to do in this new way. That also doesn't mean that everyone gets what they want from the approaches we are sharing. We'll get into this more in future chapters; however, leadership also means having hard conversations and knowing when the answer is to use a collaborative approach as compared to a decision that just has to be made by a leader. One of our hardest lessons learned when changing how we operated was learning that we can't make every decision collaboratively and that we have to assess which decisions call for certain processes or actions. Learning that the power is in the process (Chapter 2) and that the steps to collaboration are often "not so easy" (Chapter 3) also means that we have to constantly assess the right approach for the situation we are in.

As you read the chapters of this book, we hope that you are offered some ideas on how to shift your thinking from solving for the "what" in special education and instead begin solving for the "how." If we can shift our approach from a viewpoint of challenges in special education that need to be fought and move instead to view such challenges as communications that help us confront the work differently, then we can begin to address the impossible work ahead of us. If we can address what we see with true partners and various competing viewpoints and collaborate on creative solutions, we can begin to make long-lasting changes to our systems. By adopting a framework of authentic collaboration, schools and districts can begin to see meaningful change within their existing structures. It is by offering a seat to those who are not historically invited to our education table and by honoring their expertise that we can have the courage to see successful and collaborative changes in special education.

Closing Activity

We'll end each chapter with an activity that you can reproduce and complete. This will help you engage with the content chapter by chapter and begin to redesign special education at your school or district with distinct actions as you read.

Ground Yourself in Your "Why"

If you've picked up this book, you have a story to tell about why you want to be a special education leader. This work is hard (sometimes impossible), and this chapter notes that most leaders do this work because they have a vision of change that they want to actualize. Take a moment to ground in why you are doing this work and what your vision is as a special education leader.

Why do I choose to be a special education leader? What's my story?

What is the vision of change I want to actualize in my career?

Note

1 U.S. Department of Education, Office of Special Education Programs, "OSEP Fast Facts: IDEA 45th Anniversary" *IDEA Individuals with Disabilities Education Act*. Last modified May 26, 2023, Accessed on June 16, 2023, https://sites.ed.gov/idea/osep-fast-facts-idea-45th-anniversary/

References

A History of the Individuals with Disabilities Education Act, 2023, January 11. Retrieved from https://sites.ed.gov/idea/IDEA-History

Finn, C., Rotherham, A., & Hokanson, C. (2001). *Rethinking Special Education for a New Century*. Thomas B. Fordham Foundation and the Progressive Policy Institute.

2

The Power Is in the Process

As educational consultants, we often get teacher or mentee requests to share documents. For example, we often get asked to share our behavioral handbook by neighboring districts and providers. Likewise, when we are stuck, it often feels like if we could locate a rubric or preexisting document, our current problem would be solved. After making the mistake of sharing these items or attempting to implement others' frameworks, we have learned that the power is in the process. The hazard of prescribing plans, frameworks or rubrics is that doing so often causes the item to live on the shelf and never be put into practice. Context matters. Working with teams and navigating the cognitive dissonance of a problem are as necessary as the outcomes in most scenarios. We have seen initiative after initiative fail because the proper effort was not put into stakeholder dialogue, craftsmanship and buy-in. In an effort to help expand on this principle, we will give you some historical context and walk you through a process you might replicate.

In 2014, we decided to introduce board-certified behavior analysts (BCBAs) to our district. It was a new professional discipline that had not traditionally existed in educational-based special education departments. Special education teams have consisted of a teacher, psychologist or social worker, speech pathologist and occupational therapist for decades. Decisions in educational systems are often made slowly and without linear progress, and so, true to form, the budget approval and hiring for the BCBAs proceeded the conceptualization of this position and defining of the role. It wasn't long before we began to experience tension from overlapping disciplines, such as counselors, psychologists and social workers, related to the fit of this discipline into our multidisciplinary team. All of the aforementioned professions participated previously in functional behavior assessments and the development of behavior support plans. What was their role with the addition of behavior analysts to a team? What overlaps, and what would change? Who wrote the plan? Monitored a plan? Took the lead expert or made a final decision? Additionally, we had very vocal outside provider and advocacy groups who expect their clients to receive similar support from school to school. There was conflict within schools and teams, as well as in the community, and everyone demanded answers. The concept of adding behavior analysts to the team was strong; however, the implementation and change management needed work in its first years. It became clear that we needed to build a process by which each provider had a clear and distinct role, and a process that would have some consistency along the continuum. Oh yeah, and we needed to do that while we already had professionals hired and doing the work.

Our traditional special education system would have had these authors sit in a room, develop a guide and begin dictating the role of each professional on the team. We would have updated the role of the speech-language pathologist (SLP) and the special education teacher, written a beautiful roles and responsibilities guide and then rolled it out from the top down at the next professional learning event. This would work and has been mostly effective time and time again at providing a solution to a complex challenge. However, this book is about redesigning special education, and the redesigned solution is a process that has significantly more power and depth for impact.

As leaders for the various involved groups, we decided that the redesigned solution was to form a committee and use collaborative learning to develop a solution. The committee was tasked with designing a handbook that would guide providers through the process of doing a Functional Behavioral Analysis (FBA) and writing a Behavior Support Plan (BSP). We knew that we wanted a single product that all groups could use, but we also knew that BCBAs were writing clinical plans, whereas a counselor might want to do a less formal behavior plan or contract. Each group had slightly different theoretical paradigms, and each discipline had some initial tension about the newly hired disciplines placed in the field. We also knew we didn't want three separate products or to make one group feel dismissed. Notably, the task wasn't to design the roles and tasks of the team members. By creating a focus on a more complex task—the product—the committee had to struggle with roles, paradigms, beliefs and more to create a cohesive product guide.

We hesitantly set off to create a multidisciplinary team of stakeholders to build this handbook, with trepidation that any agreement would be reached. We began soliciting committee members, with the forethought to invite at least two participants from each group and began to think about how to organize the expertise and voices of participants. How could we utilize group contingencies in order to both create a product with buy-in but also grow the capacity of participants to fully understand the content? How could we ensure that the new discipline of content experts (behavior analysts) would assimilate into the system of educational setting experts (special service providers)? Finally, how would we merge varying theoretical underpinnings into one working practice? As we planned, we focused on the power of teaching to improve retention and learning of information. The following visual continuously presented itself (Table 2.1).

TABLE 2.1 Learning Activity Compared to Retention of Knowledge

Knowledge Retention Rate (%)	*Learning Activity*
90%	**Teach** someone else/use immediately.
75%	**Practice** what one learned.
50%	Engage in a **group discussion**.
30%	**Watch a demonstration.**
20%	**Watch audiovisual.**
10%	**Read.**
5%	Listen to a **lecture.**

We envisioned different means to the same end and how we might mobilize our committee accordingly. If we had each group offer an overview of their profession in a lecture or discussion format, while each group might listen, individuals may also just be focused on what they would present about their own profession. Organizing the committee in this way may grow understanding about the various profession's practice models, but it also might inadvertently strengthen the pronounced difference and end up with more passive engagement. If we approached this task with a demonstration by sharing existing content in the field, it might result in a glorified wordsmithing or adoption of an existing framework that did not formally fit the context of our setting. We really had to ponder: What was the right approach? We also did not want to reinvent the wheel, knowing that the science of behavior is evidence based—a concept our new behavior analysts would be certain to highlight. With backward planning, we settled on a skeleton of the product to include topics like introduction, understanding setting events, functions of behavior, common terms in behavior and reinforcement. We made sure that all of the controversial topics that emerged in the blending of the two fields were covered. We then created subcommittees for two to three people from varying disciplines to research, develop and teach their assigned area to the group.

We didn't know it at the time, but assigning the task of teaching to the group actually set the process of learning into motion. Suddenly, all of the egos retreated, as both groups were charged with teaching a shared topic to the group at large. In order to teach content, you are forced to learn it. Teaching a topic requires you to consider different learner's perspectives and that you master the content. It requires that you be prepared to answer questions that a variety of learners might have. It requires that you consider resistance or barriers to understanding.

After each subgroup had an opportunity to research, read the latest evidence related to their topic and draft content, they came back to the larger group to share. We then set out to draft and finalize a product, which was our original endeavor. Because of the process, the handbook was successfully introduced to the larger provider groups and is still in use today. It likely is very similar to a handbook or guide that would have been created and prescribed by our leadership team if we had done it ourselves, but the power was in the PROCESS. It took longer, took more planning, had more conflict, but ultimately, the PROCESS is why it is now in practice nearly ten years later.

> **BOX 2.1   Process Implemented: Multidisciplinary Product Creation**
> - Identify the objective or area for guidance.
> - Identify the collaboration group composition and time line needed.
> - Propose subsections for the end product.
> - Work in subcommittees to research.
> - Develop and teach each subsection to the group.
> - Draft and finalize the product by subsection.
> - Present new product to larger system.

In addition to our original outcome, we achieved unintended positive outcomes.

We grew the overall expertise of our psychologists, social workers and behavior analysts of the best practices in the field. Each subgroup became mini experts on their topic and was exposed to the most up-to-date evidence and expert opinions in their areas. Many of the group might not have been exposed to behavioral literature since graduate school, and the learning experience elevated everyone as experts.

While site-based providers might not feel as comfortable asking for help from district personnel, they now had a group of trusted colleagues who had the capacity to help them along with an FBA or behavior plan—essentially a teacher leader. In doing this work, we began to define the roles of the multidisciplinary team members, and we developed group leaders who would positively develop those roles with their larger teams.

We enhanced both the collaboration between and understanding of the roles of psychologists, social workers, SLPs, counselors and behavior analysts. Not only did they gain an understanding of another's unique perspectives, but they also somewhat developed a multitiered continuum of support from less to most clinical interventions and how they each might interface with the product in their distinct role.

We ended up with an FBA/BSP handbook that effectively meets all of our needs. It has hyperlinked tools and examples for those who would like to take a deep dive into specific topics but also has basic and more informal information for those who are using it to inform more basic behavior contracts or strategies.

With the exception of our original outcome, we did not plan on any of these amazing by-products. We did not set out to accomplish any of the things noted earlier. We also would not be able to predict that they would happen. It was only in reflection and allowing the task to be a PROCESS that these things happened. We still were able to get to our end goal, but the stakeholders guided the process.

As a leader, are you brave enough to trust the process? Can you step into a committee or work group and trust that your agenda or needs will be met? Can you allow your staff the same space to think around a topic and formulate conclusions, maybe even teach you? Are you willing to take the risk to let go of control and possibly fail in your intended objective and to take the risk that by engaging with teams in the process, your collaboration might end up better than you had originally planned?

A School-Based Scenario

These last few pages described a large, systemwide process. Yet, what about our readers who are leading special education teams at the school level? We also think the same principles of redesign can apply to work at a school or an example on a smaller scale.

Just recently, we were involved in a request from a parent who wanted their child's schedule changed at a middle school. The school and district followed the usual traditional special education protocol. The principal let the family know that the teacher would address the concern at the lowest level, and the teacher, along with the psychologist, wrote up a list of expectations for the student. They reviewed the expectations with the student, let him know that the class would not change and told him that he needed to begin doing his math work in the current support class. They crafted a contract with the student with clear expectations, and within a day or two, the problem was "solved," as a response had been given. Check-task complete. That is until a few months later when the student was refusing to do all tasks, and the relationship between the student and staff had deteriorated completely.

We'll admit that once the process in the previous paragraph failed, we deployed a more collaborative and committee-style process and landed on a much different outcome through the leadership of the principal who was leading the special education team at the school.

In response to the change in schedule, the principal, director of special education, special education teacher, psychologist, parent, student and outside tutor all came to a meeting to collaborate. This wasn't an IEP meeting; rather, it was a discussion of how an IEP service was to be implemented in a scenario where the student was refusing to engage in the existing schedule.

You may first ask, why did the outside tutor come to the meeting? They attended because they had expertise regarding times when the student was highly engaged in math. They saw what he could do in math, how and when he got frustrated and had discussed with the student why he was refusing in school. You may also ask, why was the special education director involved? This is a school-based decision that wouldn't require district leadership to attend or make a decision; however, in this case, the director had a long-standing relationship with both the school and the family. They knew how hard it was for this student to get "unstuck" once things had eroded and how important relationships were to finding successful solutions for this student in particular, and they could offer up unique ideas or possible resources. By adding some unexpected experts to this discussion, we were able to add unexpected perspectives that might help us find solutions.

The meeting convened in a virtual setting with no agenda. The principal had organized the group, set the meeting time and began the collaboration by posing a simple question—what can we do to address the student's need for math services? Each person was given the time to explain what they knew about the current situation and to add to a definition of the problem. Let us remind you that the student was in this conversation. The student shared their perspective, was a valued member of the team AND was able to hear caring adults share their concerns and hopes. This was quite different from the first and traditional solution, the one where the student was told what he was to do next to comply and engage. Would you agree that there is power in this new process? What would be different for the student in this approach?

The first part of the process took over 45 minutes. By this point, we were a little worried about time and if we would get anywhere with the process, but we had the courage to keep going and try. Next, the special education teacher thanked everyone for helping them to understand what was going on from their perspective. She then asked the group to write on a document any idea that they had for achieving the best hopes for this student and address the need for math services. Each person had an opportunity to write down an idea or two. The group then had a chance to read the ideas. The special education teacher then asked if any of the possible solutions needed more research or more clarification. Quickly, the student spoke up and asked why we could not just offer him a study hall. He wanted a break in his day and explained how long it was for him to attend for a full seven hours. He was overwhelmed and felt that he could not engage in another 50-minute period of work. After a quick discussion, another member asked to clarify another option that proposed a new individual. The principal shared that there was a math tutor in the building who could be an option to help with some math services. The discussion continued for about ten minutes regarding various proposals. At a lull, the principal summarized that the group seemed to be leaning toward a 25-minute block with the math tutor in a very small group and then a 30-minute break for the student. This addressed what the student needed to make it through the day, resolved the need for math services and also addressed the relationship challenge that had grown with the current teacher. The principal asked if there was any disagreement with the proposed plan. Hearing none, there was a quick summary of next steps (including an IEP amendment), along with time lines before the meeting ended.

> **BOX 2.2   Process Implemented: Expert Problem-Solving**
> - Identify the problem to be solved.
> - Convene a group of experts who have information and varied viewpoints regarding the problem to be solved.
> - Provide time for each expert to share information.
> - Write down possible proposals to address the problem.
> - Discuss and research proposals for feasibility.
> - Propose and explore one possible solution.
> - Summarize next steps.

A few days later, the student began the new plan. He felt empowered to engage in the math services because he had participated in and owned the decision-making process. Additionally, he felt valued and cared for in the process, which resulted in renewed positive engagements at school moving forward. The teacher had been concerned because of how disruptive the student had been, and now her class was free of distraction, and other students could learn. The process took longer than the traditional approach; however, the outcomes were much deeper and long-lasting for all involved.

What Is the Process?

If you are now interested in redesigning special education through collaborative processes similar to those scenarios shared earlier in this chapter, you are most likely wondering what process to use. We'll discuss more about the steps for collaborative processes in Chapter 3 from a broad lens. In terms of a protocol, unfortunately, there is not one right process for every scenario. Remember that we started this chapter by noting that it can be a mistake to share a framework or protocol because the process matters. The leader of the process needs to be a curator of collaboration who is willing to design the time and the membership needed to get to an outcome. They curate the specialized process needed for the unique scenario and needs. We are sharing some sample steps of processes that we have created throughout this book as a guide for thinking, and we continue to encourage readers to spend time as the designer for what will work best for their unique needs.

There are many formal processes out there that could be used as references for planning. Some of our favorites include Bob Chadwick's *Finding New Ground*[1] and the related article, "Beyond Conflict to Consensus."[2] This is an excellent resource for true consensus building and shared decision-making with a focus on conflict resolution. We also frequently reference Adaptive Schools,[3] which has extensive strategies and protocols with various collaborative intents, much available for free at their website thinkingcollaborative.com. Lastly, we'd refer you to the *Design Thinking Handbook,* which is available online for free and is a guide that focuses on a user-centered perspective that is an iterative system with many variations.[4] We use some of these frameworks as reference when we want to generate and create new and innovative solutions with our collaborative teams.

As each leader, challenge and team is different, we will offer up some questions for you to consider as you curate your process:

- What is the problem you are trying to solve? Do we all understand the problem the same way, or do we need to spend time defining it together?
- Who needs to be at the collaborative table? Who will be there that can offer some unexpected perspectives and stretch the thinking (more in Chapter 4)?
- Do you need to spend time developing the group, introducing each other, setting norms for authentic listening?
- Do you need to understand the worst fears and best hopes of the group?
- For emotionally charged topics, do we need to spend time listening and reflecting various perspectives before moving to problem-solving?
- Do you need an agenda? Or is this a topic that the group can design a process around the challenge?

- What is the intended outcome? Are we seeking consensus, developing a product, designing a solution?
- Will there be a need to research ideas? Brainstorm creative solutions?
- How will you ensure all voices are heard?
- What is the role of small groups?

As the facilitator of the process, plan to spend more time than you'd expect such that everyone has a chance to be heard. We are always surprised at how much time a true collaborative process takes. If you think it's going to take 30 minutes, we suggest scheduling 90 minutes. If you think it'll take three meetings, plan twice as many and cancel if needed. (Facilitator tip—everyone is always happier when you're done early or cancel a scheduled meeting rather than adding on a meeting because the work wasn't done in time.)

Next, come to the table knowing that you are guiding the process and that you will need to let go of the outcome. Early on, we discovered that the beauty of the collaborative process is letting go and not having to have all the answers (more in Chapter 6). This also means that you cannot control the outcome. Too many times, we've gone into a committee or an IEP meeting, certain that we have to determine a specific outcome because it is the absolute best decision, and we've been left gobsmacked that the actual decision was something completely different. For individuals new to being collaboration curators, this is both freeing and terrifying. You will need to come in with a plan and learn to abandon it as the group takes things in various directions. You'll come to the table and often listen without even participating. And you'll eventually find the courage to sit back and recognize the beauty and power that these practices will have to create change.

Along with the guiding questions, our scenarios throughout the book can give you some guiding ideas for approaches. The following is one sample agenda and process that was used for a meeting at a school. This was used after an IEP meeting for an incredibly unique student who was not able to attend the regular summer program. The family was insistent that the district needed to fund something very specialized for the summer. The student didn't want to give up his summer for school and was generally resistant to any summer learning. The IEP team had specific regression and recoupment data indicating eligibility for Extended School Year (ESY) in the area of social skills. The director of special education was working from a limited budget and was worried about being able to fund a unique plan. The IEP meeting was held, and the conflict was discovered. After several minutes of arguing at the IEP meeting, the director suggested a follow-up meeting to create a student-specific ESY plan that addressed all the voices in the room. The director of special education was the facilitator of the agenda.

BOX 2.3   Sample Agenda: ESY Planning Meeting

Participants: Parent, advocate, general education teacher, special education teacher, special education director, principal, BCBA, SLP, student

Time: 90 minutes

Agenda

1. Define the problem we are trying to solve: create a unique and individualized ESY plan for (student) that meets the skill maintenance requirements for his social skills goal.
2. Participants introduce themselves with their name, their role today and what they hope for the student this summer.
3. Brainstorm a list of criteria to meet for the proposed solution (actual criteria listed).
    a. Address maintenance of social goal
    b. High interest, so student will want to attend
    c. Reasonable—meaning affordable and available
    d. Safe access can be provided
4. Brainstorm any and all possible ideas that could meet the criteria on whiteboard.
5. Participants put a checkmark next to their favorite idea.
6. Prioritized ideas are discussed with student feedback.
7. Summarize decisions and next steps.

In case you are wondering about the results of this agenda, the group decided that the student should go to a ten-day Lego engineering camp at the local university for his ESY program. The student was highly interested. The camp was funded by the district, and a paraeducator was able to attend with the student for safety due to his potential for aggressive behavior. The cost of the 60 hours of camp was similar to the cost of the previously unsuccessful partial day six-week ESY program; however, it was more likely to produce specific outcomes for social interaction due to the interest and social groups available at the camp. This was a model that was used for several summers with this student until he showed improvements and was able to attend more independently without a paraeducator.

The unintended outcomes of this process included positive relationships that were developed with the family and the advocate. They saw the district's willingness to come to the table to problem-solve unique challenges. This also allowed for real dialogue regarding cost and safety that might not have been able to be discussed so openly prior to this process. The teachers, who had previously been concerned about litigation with this family, felt a release of pressure and responsibility to have all of the answers. The student felt so empowered that he began attending his own IEP meetings as he learned that he had a voice that could be heard. Two years later, he came to his IEP meeting and asked to "hack the IEP process" and redesign school to work for him. The team sat back and let him take over.

By redesigning the special education process, either at the school or district level, we can embrace collaboration. We can celebrate that collaboration allows us to listen to many competing voices, often the voices that can be in strong, contentious conflict, and borrow the very best ideas to make something new and better than any one person could have possibly created. In doing so, we also create partnerships in the decisions that are made. These partnerships build relationships and trust and often result in deeper, longer-term solutions for both staff and families.

Closing Activity

Self-Interview: The Power Is in the Process

List three processes that you use now that could be redesigned with collaboration.

Identify three areas that would not be appropriate to use collaborative processes. Why are these different?

Identify any individuals you need to talk to next about making the changes in question one.

How can you address the time needed for redesigning one or more of the processes identified earlier?

Write your action steps to try a more collaborative process in one of the areas you noted over the next few weeks. Write them down and commit to them!

Revisit this interview once you've tried a process or two. Write your reflection below. Was the process freeing or frightening? What worked well? What surprised you? What will you do differently next time?

Notes

1 Chadwick, Robert J., *Finding New Ground: Beyond Conflict to Consensus*, Oregon, One Tree Publishing Company, 2012.
2 Chadwick, Bob, *Beyond Conflict to Consensus: An Introductory Learning Manual*, Last modified n.d., Accessed on June 16, 2023, https://managingwholes.com/chadwick.htm/
3 Garmston, Robert J. and Wellman, Bruce M., *The Adaptive School*, Dallas, Texas, Maryland, Rowman and Littlefield, 2016, https://www-origin.abebooks.com/servlet/BookDetailsPL?bi=31589587540&searchurl=an%3Dgarmston%2Bco%2Bdeveloper%2Bcognitive%2Bcoaching%2Badaptive%26ds%3D10%26sortby%3D17&cm_sp=msrp-_-msrpdesc-_-bdp
4 Woolery, Eili, *Design Thinking Handbook*, Last modified n.d., Accessed on June 16, 2023, https://www.designbetter.co/design-thinking

3

Six Not-So-Easy Steps for Collaborative Change

Collaboration is not easy. Change is also never easy and always full of its own challenges. Put those together, and the collaborative approaches offered in this book can be hard to implement. Add to that the cognitive process of letting go of old systems, and you'll find a messy web of interwoven needs that are hard to begin to address. We are not here to ask you to implement something new because it will be easier. The burden of special education leaders is huge and getting bigger by the day. We are constantly jumping from one conflict to another. These are "not-so-easy" steps because the process can be difficult on many levels. And yet, what we have found is that this way of working as special education leaders has many more positive, long-term and systematic impacts. Time and hard work can even resolve many future concerns that you don't even know will exist.

To make the work a little bit easier, this chapter hopes to provide six steps that could be followed as a guide for those learning how to develop authentic collaborations at any level of the system. This is not a recipe or a guidebook (keep in mind our process message in Chapter 2) but rather steps or concepts that can frame this shift in thinking.

Step 1: Dive into the Problem and Seek to Understand

This first step really requires the art of listening. Whether you agree or not, just listen to understand. Listen to those who have concerns without needing to defend or respond and ask lots of questions. Ask for the data. Ask for the stories and try to understand the various perspectives involved. Ask the question and bring a notepad to write down what you hear. Ask clarifying questions and frequently restate what you hear. This is not the time to discuss solutions or respond with your views. It is not the time to say whether you agree or disagree. The point is just to listen.

Around 2016, our district was seeing increased concerns around students with reading disabilities. Families were calling, and community groups were organizing. It became clear that our literacy practices were not in alignment with what families wanted for their children. Our Literacy Department felt confident that they were doing what was best for students, and special education leaders felt confident that we were following the rules and regulations that we are so deeply guided by. And yet, at every board meeting, parents would speak up with concerns. Nearly every day, we would get calls asking for something different or complaining about what we did not have available. Advocates began asking for more and more compensatory education services, and community groups began organizing—all around the area of reading. At a state-level special education meeting, our department leaders sat down and began to discuss the statewide lack of progress for students with specific learning disabilities (SLD). We looked at each other across the table and could acknowledge that there was a giant problem to solve, and we were not sure where to begin.

We left that day with the stark realization that the implementation of reading services was important but never had raised to the level of urgency for our small district-level special education leaders. We spent so much time addressing the urgent items, the crisis needs, that some of our most important items were not being given time.

We left committed to starting to address this need and finding out how we could even begin. Intuitively, here is where a special education director might go into their office, order up the most up-to-date book or resource and start working on an implementation plan to roll out at next year's professional learning day. Our plan was going to take much more time and effort, and, hopefully, have much more lasting impact.

First, we needed to really understand the problem. We listened that day to the Colorado Department of Education leaders and then decided to reorganize our department to have instructional leaders who would have key roles in addressing instructional needs moving forward. We did not add one penny to the budget—we shifted the roles from everyone who was addressing urgent issues to having "chief worriers" who were now going to address the important instructional issues for the team.

Next, those individuals had to spend time seeking to understand. We began by creating a list of those we needed to meet with in order to understand perspectives. Literacy director, literacy interventionists, special education teachers, principals—the list began with district staff. Then we moved on to those who would have more conflicting opinions, including local advocates, parents, community groups and student's themselves. Over a series of months, we got ourselves to a lot of tables and just listened.

This part was actually incredibly hard because we came with our own biases and needs. We were listening to various voices while we were still getting urgent phone calls and demands for compensatory education. But we could not solve the system problems until we understood them at a deep level. We did have to solve individual needs during that time while we worked on the longer-term system challenges. Oftentimes, we are taxed as leaders to find and implement temporary solutions while simultaneously being charged with solving a larger problem.

We sat in meetings where we heard attacks on our staff and the district. We heard how many people believed that we did not care about students, that we were blind to the lack of progress and that we were essentially failing students and harming our community. Reminder to our readers here that it often takes courage to listen, especially when the content is deeply emotional and disparate beliefs. Yet, no one is harmed by simply listening. We sat in meetings where educators shared beliefs about students that were completely contrary to what we believed. Although there were also many positive things shared, it was important that we just spent time hearing what was going on from all the perspectives.

What we came to understand is that the key concern from the community was around students with dyslexia and other language-based learning disabilities and that our district was not implementing evidence-based reading practices that would address their needs. Our district, on the other hand, believed that they were following all the requirements and doing what they were taught and trained to do that was best for teaching reading. The conflict was huge and, come to find out, becoming a national divide.

Step 2: Seek Partnerships in the Community Groups That Are Involved

We have lived the experience of many community groups coming together with a purpose, and the very best way to address the needs of special education is to ally with our community, have coffee with advocates and share cell phone numbers, go to events for community groups, attend their conferences, read their books and bring together an advisory committee that includes their views. We believe deeply and strongly that we cannot solve these ever-evolving challenges in special education without these community partners.

As we began to understand the conflict in our community around students with dyslexia, we had to seek partnerships in the community. This began in a not-so-positive way when our local dyslexia group asked for a meeting and notified us that they would be bringing a lawyer to the conversation.

We all sat in the meeting and uncomfortably discussed information. We were eventually able to have special education leaders kindly remark that we cannot offer creative solutions and partnerships when lawyers are monitoring our conversations. We asked if we could meet another time and bring in more leaders to begin a process of collaboration.

Now, we won't claim that these next steps were smooth, as they were not. It took strong leadership and real trust in a collaborative process to navigate these next steps. It also took a directive from our superintendent to create a committee with community leaders and district leaders who could sit down and start to work together. We would not advise allowing conflict to rise to that level, yet the truth is that sometimes it gets elevated and out of control.

After the meeting with lawyers, we brought together our literacy leaders, special education leaders and community group leaders. At their request, we also involved some community advocates and representatives from the International Dyslexia Association (IDA). For those who are already having hairs raised with the idea that advocates and national organization representatives were part of the meetings and could cause deeper conflict, let me skip to the end and tell you that these individuals often helped support the district through some of the deepest divides, and we are forever grateful for their participation. You'll hear this theme throughout the book: by bringing in those different and opposing voices, we can often create better solutions, and that is very true of this group.

We had a few meetings and discussions and then eventually began to form an advisory group called the Dyslexia Advisory Group. This group was co-led by the director of special education and the director of literacy, as well as two community leaders representing our parent group. We spent weeks discussing a process and protocol to use for a first meeting. We discussed if we needed a facilitator. We discussed arduously who would be in the group. Ultimately, we landed on about eight district representatives, including teachers, principals and literacy coaches and then a similar number of parents and IDA representatives. We also decided that the first meeting needed to be facilitated and focused on listening to the deeply embedded sides of the conflict and getting to know each other as people.

About 11 pm the night before the meeting, things almost fell apart. The Literacy Director called the special education leader (one of the authors) nearly ready to give up and completely worried about the event. One of the community leaders called about ten minutes later, concerned that we were taking the wrong approach and asking to cancel the meeting and change the agenda to a plan where we just started solving the problem. I remember sitting on my stairs with my family asleep and the house completely dark, just repeating the mantra to myself that we would not allow this to crumble. In each call, I calmly quoted the evidence for the approach we were going to use and asked for a small amount of trust to let us try this first step.

The next morning, we sat in a circle, introduced ourselves and began the work. We were asked to share our best hopes and worst fears (see Bob Chadwick's *Finding New Ground* for a reference of our process.) In rereading the worst fears that we documented so many years ago, I can still feel the pain from that meeting and how much hurt was brought into the group. Worst fears included the following:

- Children and families will continue to suffer.
- Any inequity in our district of the haves and the have-nots (will) continue.
- (If nothing changes, we will continue to have) devastating mental health issues for dyslexic kids and their families.
- Anger will increase in the community against the district and continue to cause huge issues with mistrust.
- More students graduate feeling horrible about their skills and without being able to read.
- Thousands of children fail to realize their potential.

- Many families will be literally destroyed.
- The number of times that this group calls out our district negatively on Facebook is too much. We do a lot of great things in our district, and to constantly be called out negatively has to stop.

Our facilitator put us in groups to discuss what we wrote, and I recall hearing people yell and cry from across the room. I recall walking out of the building that day and a teacher crying to me on the stairway down to our cars, sharing that this was too deep and too intense because they cared so much for the students and were doing what they knew was best. They couldn't believe that there was so much hurt in the community.

As impossibly hard as this was and will be in some of our deepest needs in special education, the partnership and involvement of those voices in the community were ultimately absolutely necessary to the long-term solutions for our students. When work becomes emotional, it could be easy to stop here—I've seen many leaders close the doors and just work in isolation when we get to some of these biggest challenges. We encourage you not to stop when you hit this critical point. The chapter is labeled with "not-so-easy" steps for a reason, and working through this dissonance and voicing of conflict will allow you to move into the next phase more collaboratively.

Step 3: Set Goals for Change

I always tell people that we are special educators, and we can't help but set goals for everything. The IEP process is a beautiful thing, and the process can work in many areas, including work between adults. Being clear about the targets and quantifying them is critical. If you don't know where you're headed when you leave the house and go down the road, will you end up at the right place? Probably not. The same is true for leadership. I've also learned over time that you do not have to have the plan to accomplish the goal when you set it. Often, we don't even know where to start. Setting the goal is the start.

Our dyslexia group gave ourselves the title of the Dyslexia Advisory Team or DAT. After our first meeting, we somehow all went back into the room and started to focus on our best hopes. Now that we worked through the emotions and depth of what we were all bringing to the conversation, we could begin to focus on our hopes for the work and set some goals. The hopes were the exact opposite of the fears, noting things like the following:

- Students will gain self-confidence.
- Teachers will have the knowledge to improve student outcomes.
- District-wide knowledge and training around dyslexia.
- Students become adults who are successful and full of joy.

The entire second meeting was now able to be focused on vision and goals. This was no easy task because the goals of one group were vastly different from the goals of the other. We started with a vision statement and had to argue every word. We continually asked if there was any disagreement and revised from there. It was a painful process. I kid you not; every word was scrutinized and manipulated until we had a plan we could at least say had "no disagreement."[1] Leadership note here: seeking agreement is a way different thing than asking if there is any disagreement. It's the language I live by when we are making hard decisions.

In two hours, we finally agreed to two sentences. First was the vision of the DAT group, and second were four areas we agreed could be the focus of the advisory. We now had a clear and collective goal that every meeting and years of work could align to.

Step 4: Figure Out What It Is Going to Take to Meet Those Goals

It's a myth that you can't commit to something that you don't have the answer for. Sometimes you do the best work by committing to solve and figuring out how after. Sometimes you have to just ask, "What if we could?" and take the first steps to solve something that hasn't been solved before.

Once our dyslexia group had a vision or goal, we realized we had no idea what the path was to accomplish the goal. We now had a group of people committed to the work, and we had to figure out what came next.

Over the summer following our first meeting, the leaders of the group met and created a plan. We set up monthly meetings and solidified our participants. We also identified some guests who would need to join. For example, we needed our director who oversaw assessment to be able to explain information about common assessments so that we could discuss how we might measure outcomes. We needed another director to join to share information about Multitiered Systems of Support and yet another director to share the work that special education was doing. We quickly realized that the first steps were going to be learning and identifying the current state in the four areas that we agreed to be advisory for. We also realized that we needed to set the expectation that the work would be focused on a three- to five-year plan for change.

We spent several meetings setting norms, time lines and structures, and then we identified what the current state was in each of our four areas of work. Over the next several agendas, we began to focus on the next stage of the work, asking what steps we could take in 2017–18 to further this work. Lastly, we began a long list of questions that needed to be answered in the work ahead.

Very slowly, a map began to emerge about how we could achieve these goals. As leaders in special education, we began to see where we were going to be able to improve and how we could work alongside our community to advocate for the funds and time to make those improvements. All of a sudden, the work became exciting and hopeful, and we could see so many positives ahead.

As another leadership note, the challenge at this phase started to become the pacing. As special education leaders, we often have to remind ourselves that change in education is very often slow.

We know that the next time for professional learning or budget development or hiring new staff is often far in the future. We plan ahead for system changes and know that is the way of many systems. For community members, this is not innate knowledge. Our committee had to constantly remind ourselves that the work was now moving forward and that the pacing would be slower than we had wanted.

As a reminder, when we say *our committee*, this process was co-led by two district leaders and two community representatives. We shared the leadership and balanced the power to ensure all voices were heard. In between each committee meeting, the co-leaders met to debrief the prior meeting, review the next agenda and then strategize for what was next.

Step 5: Have the Hard Conversations and Make the Changes Needed

As change begins to happen, often hard conversations become necessary to move the work forward. As leaders of special education in a school or at the department level, we have to have the grit to have these hard conversations to move the work forward. This could be a conversation with a resistant staff member or team. It could be work to move the budget from one priority to another and inform a group that their work won't be funded any longer. It might be a conversation that certain practices are no longer going to be supported or any other variety of change implementation.

In terms of our DAT work, special education quickly proceeded with a materials adoption process and purchasing evidence-based resources for reading interventions for students on IEPs. The work was exciting as we collaboratively went through the adoption process, including community members, advocates and students, and landed on some unexpected results.

What came next was a series of surprisingly hard conversations. At the start of the following school year, we began rolling out the training for the new reading interventions. Although most staff were thrilled with the depth of information and their newly found ability to respond to parents' and also students' needs, there was some resistance. We took the stance that the Orton-Gillingham-based intervention was our core intervention in basic reading/decoding. Given that every school had students with basic reading needs, we required each school to have at least one group utilizing this intervention. Most schools proceeded, followed the rules, reported out their data and moved forward with the systems change. As they saw representation on the DAT committee and on the adoption process, they felt a part of the change and were able to move forward.

At a few schools, staff were not as on board. We had several staff members who refused to attend training and several schools that refused to move to the new intervention. In the first year, we moved ahead and did not communicate much with those who were resistant to the change. In the second year, we had to have more accountability and began reaching out to those who were not implementing. There were a lot of reasons for resistance to the change, but ultimately, time and time again, we had families who were insisting that an Orton-Gillingham-based intervention was to be used, and data on other interventions, at least in the area of decoding, were not providing the same type of results. Our special education directors had to have hard conversations with principals and teachers to make it clear that our expectations were to complete the training and use evidence-based intervention for the students with those needs.

Years into the implementation of this work, there have been many hard conversations to be had. We've had to say no to certain assessments that were requested by our community because they were not the right fit for our system and would be too much of a burden on the assessment system that existed. It was hard to say after finally coming together and making so much progress; however, it was the right thing to do in the process. We also had many hard conversations about teachers and leaders who were not the right fit for the work we were doing. We had many staff leave for different positions or districts because this was not aligned with the work they wanted to do. Ultimately, we began carrying the message that this was the direction of the district, and it was moving forward.

The result of the steps shared so far was massive, multiyear, systematic change. Although this book is about special education leadership, this change was made deeply in both special education and general education. Those meetings where we yelled and cried faded away and were replaced by true partnerships between school and community. We began supporting each other in how we brought in families who had students in need. Our messages began to be more common and aligned. We stopped having upset families at the board meetings and daily phone calls from advocates with concerns. Instead, we saw multilevel shifts in how we implemented reading instruction and data that showed students were making improvements in their ability to read.

Step 6: Don't Stop There

The success we might see after step 5 could be a good place to end the story (and the chapter), and yet it is important to ensure leaders in special education don't stop there. Keep those relationships and continue to partner. Often, the deep work that needs to be done continues for years and decades and just takes on new shapes and forms. Not to mention that the next conflict is right around the corner, waiting to be a learning opportunity.

For some of these areas of need, it is as simple as continuing the committee work even when most of the goals are met. Continue going to the Autism Society events and meeting with that community agency point of contact. Continue the partnership with the Down Syndrome Association. Create a monthly advocate meeting to have a system for proactive feedback. The frequency and intensity of the collaboration might change, and yet the connection is still needed even as you start to meet your objectives of the work.

Our DAT group continued on for years and is continuing as we publish this book. Most of those initial goals and visions were met in our three- to five-year plan, and now the work is evolving. Now we are looking at the data and need to make adjustments to implementation to see more growth. We need to look at our work for students who are learning English and have dyslexia. We are considering updating our universal instructional materials. We are exploring what more we can do for students with mild intellectual disabilities and those who are not responding to the systems we put in place in the way we want to see them respond. We are looking at updating our assessments. You get the idea; the work is evolving.

Just recently, there was a board meeting where a new reading material was being proposed. Because the DAT and our community were already involved and already aligned, there was only one community representative who spoke. She spoke in favor of the change. She saw the special education presentation for the night and asked the director to be clear that the data that was being presented was only around primary disability. Thirty percent of students on IEPs had a primary disability of SLD, and they wanted the community to understand that this did not capture all of those with a reading need—that others had secondary disabilities or were unidentified. The director made the note on the slides, and the meeting moved on. To most people, this was nothing of note. Who would even notice a comment for support and a comment for clarification? Those who saw where we were nearly six years before could recognize how incredible these little things were as we worked together in a unified way forward, with deep understanding and alignment.

BOX 3.1   Process Implemented: Six Steps

- Step 1 – Dive into the problem and seek to understand.
- Step 2 – Seek partnerships in the community groups that are involved.
- Step 3 – Set goals for change.
- Step 4 – Figure out what it is going to take to meet those goals.
- Step 5 – Have the hard conversations and make the changes needed.
- Step 6 – Don't stop there.

Closing Activity

Practice: Dive into the Problem and Seek to Understand

You don't need to dig into a multiyear, systemwide effort for change to practice some of the steps in this chapter. One quick and practicable step can be working on active listening to understand the needs and challenges that you face in special education. Identify an opportunity to actively listen in the coming week. This could be with a work situation or even an opportunity with family and friends. The key is that active listening is something that takes practice and self-reflection to do well. Use the following chart to rate yourself in each area and reflect on your practice.

Make a checkmark for how you rate your ability to do the following in the active listening practice opportunity	*Nope*	*Getting Close*	*Nearly Perfect*
1. Face the speaker.			
2. Attend to nonverbal cues.			
3. Don't interrupt.			
4. Listen without judgment.			
5. Show that you're listening—lean in, nod, acknowledge.			
6. Ask questions.			
7. Paraphrase and summarize.			

What are my areas of strength as an active listener?

What is an area in need of practice, and what can I do to practice this more?

Challenge activity: Do you have a challenge that you want to work on using the six not-so-easy steps? If so, what is it? Define your plan here for how to start.

Note

1 Chadwick, Robert J., *Finding New Ground: Beyond Conflict to Consensus*, Oregon, One Tree Publishing Company, 2012.

4

Leveraging Unexpected Partnerships

What has your experience been with first impressions? First impression psychology is a branch of psychology that studies the impact of first contact with others (N., Sam, 2013). When you think about your current most trusted professional relationships and then think back to your first impression of that person, how do they compare? Interestingly enough, although refined over time, my professional first judgment of colleagues seems to be off. Invariably, I would love someone in an interview who ended up performing poorly on the job or dislike an applicant who ended up being a very strong colleague. After a few of these experiences, including one where my most valued partner at work was a person I originally found to be difficult to work with, I have learned a few things. If you actively engage with the purpose of developing a partnership, you might discover some unexpected benefits and find ways to expand support for students.

Business Partnerships

In the early years of my daughter's development, I was working feverishly to develop teacher's behavioral tool kits in order to provide optimally engaging classrooms. It was the early years of Positive Behavior Intervention Supports (PBIS), and I was actively engaged in building positive behavior supports in schools. At that time, my daughters were just reaching the age where they could participate in activities and sports. I searched the web to find which activities accepted the youngest participants and came across gymnastics. After signing up my oldest daughter, I commenced sitting in a gym watching a coach interact with a group of ten girls for an hour each weekend. I watched as the young coach, likely a college student, struggled to try to gain instructional control. I was biting my tongue. There were so many crossover strategies that we utilized in the classroom that I felt might also be able to be utilized in gymnastics classes. After a few weeks, I courageously introduced myself to the owner and asked her if she formally offered professional development to her coaches. She explained that they had a weekly staff meeting and invited me to participate. She eagerly agreed to my training, and the staff enjoyed discussing their student profiles. It was rewarding to see them implement suggestions week by week, increase my understanding of the crossover between coaching and teaching, and begin to build partnerships between school and community. My love of "side hustles" was officially born, and the unexpected outcomes of these partnerships commenced.

I regularly describe myself as a connector or cross-pollinator. I would mine for best practices, collect them and share them with others. Over time, we have found partnerships in the most unexpected places. Networking relationships and developing partnerships prove to be the most valuable professional skills in my repertoire. Having a "say yes" mindset is the first step in networking. For example, when you are at a conference and have a break, do you get lost in your email, or do you take a risk and connect with a participant or the speaker? What steps might you take in order to take a risk and forge a partnership with someone you may or may not see as having a benefit to your professional work?

Outside Consultant Partnerships

In 2014, my special education director and her husband left to begin working overseas in India. They were forging a new career in Southern India and would occasionally send an email updating us on their endeavor. Although an American school in India, the school's values around inclusion and providing opportunities for students with disabilities to be educated were an area of focus. In their leadership, they were sometimes taxed with having to accept admission for one child and refuse their sibling. This was incredibly hard for them, being people who had strong, inclusive values and a history as special education leaders. Their shared vision and mission of building an inclusive international school that not only accepted but excelled with students with disabilities emerged. They knew it was possible because they had done the work in the United States. They called me and said, "We know you are good at connecting with others; we need a dream team." I was intrigued, inquired further and decided this was a once-in-a-lifetime opportunity. I had to say yes. A few months later, a multidisciplinary team and I were headed to India to help guarantee a successful transition for the first learner with a disability to enter the school. After doing so, we took additional trips to other countries to scale the process into other schools.

While these trips were incredibly valuable, their value was not for the reasons you or I might expect. Yes, the learner and staff were able to benefit from our support and staff training, but the benefit I hope to convey is that which was yielded for us personally and professionally and how that in turn benefits others.

For example, in working with international schools, we were exposed to Universal Design for Learning,[1] Adaptive Schools,[2] IB values[3] and Cognitive Coaching.[4] We encountered practitioners who had been deeply embedded in this training and developing staff in these skill sets. We sat in meetings about how to deliver our specialized content that was facilitated using these practices. Although trained as a clinical social worker, many of these concepts were novel to me but were so deeply congruent with PBIS and some of the areas of my clinical expertise.

Fast-forward a few years to when my leadership team began to identify a need for enhancing our district's coaching and consultation skills. We participated in a book study on the Adaptive Schools with hopes to further explore some of the approaches we were exposed to abroad. Upon completing the book study as a group of specialists, we decided to begin practicing some of these strategies and moves within our team leadership meetings with our special education directors. We were committed to applying what we learned in our own practice and sharing it with others. We discussed the importance of what we had learned with our leadership and not only got formal training the following year, but our district contracted the training for other departmental leaders to participate as well. Now, almost every administrator in our district has received the training, and there is evidence of its implementation district-wide. We still regularly use our international partners to coach us in problems of practice and difficult situations.

It is amazing to me that while the original target of the international work was around supporting an individual school to more efficiently include a child with a disability, the unexpected partnership and outcomes of that partnership include a department re-inventing their approach to professional development, eventually spreading to the district at large. This partnership has continued to have lasting effects that are revealing themselves over time, and we cannot wait to see what is next.

Considering Unexpected Educational Partnerships

In redesigning the way we think about special education leadership, we have to redesign how we think about partnerships for our day-to-day work. When most educators think of partners for problem-solving, they might write up a list that includes principals, department leaders, teachers, supervisors, reading specialists or district specialists. I'm hoping that parents would make it on many of our lists, as we engage parents in the IEP process and in usual communication structures. These are all experts in their own domain, with whom we should continue to partner with. And in order to redesign the way we work and have different outcomes, we also need to think bigger and outside of our usual educational boundaries.

> **BOX 4.1   Expected Partners**
>
> - Principals
> - Department leaders
> - Teachers
> - Supervisors
> - Reading specialists
> - Counselors
> - Psychologists
> - Occupational therapists
> - Speech-language pathologists
> - District specialists
> - Parents

When was the last time you thought of bringing in community members to help solve a problem in your district or school? Do you frequently include advocates, association representatives, paraprofessionals, private providers, community leaders, or others? Why or why not? When we've asked colleagues why they chose the people that they choose to problem solve with, they often refer to a group that understands educational systems and can help us move faster to solutions. They might often say they want to avoid significantly conflicting viewpoints. Why have you not included any of these individuals in your leadership work? Are the answers the same or different?

> **BOX 4.2   Unexpected Partners**
>
> - Business representatives
> - Outside consultants
> - Advocates
> - Community leaders
> - City leadership
> - Disability group
> - Paraprofessionals
> - Private community-based therapists
> - Legislators

The truth is that by involving individuals outside of our educational bubble, we invite people who think differently. They have different viewpoints, and yes, they might come with some conflicting ideas. Quite frankly, this can be a really scary leadership move. In bringing the head of the association on a really complex challenge, you risk opening yourself up to more criticism or barriers to moving the work forward. What if the work fails as a result? Yet, if it succeeds, you have your association president already working with you on change, allowing you to both avoid future hurdles and set up alignment that wasn't possible before.

By bringing the same people to the table and working with the same partners, we continue to achieve the same results. If you read Chapter 1, you know that these results are not working for us, and we need to try something else. We absolutely cannot do the work of special education leadership alone. The inclusion of these unexpected partners as allies in the work of special education leadership is where the magic happens.

Advocate Partnerships

In talking with colleagues around the country, we have noticed that advocates tend to bring a deeper reaction to our educational leaders when we ask them to consider potential partnerships; therefore, we are going to share some examples of how we have found success in working with this group of unexpected partners.

Our district has a lot of advocates who work on behalf of families. A few years back, we noticed that there was a fear of advocacy and advocates coming to meetings. Advocates would come to us to problem solve one by one, case by case, for situations they were involved in. It was exhausting for everyone. We decided that we needed to look at this as a form of communication and consider what it was telling us about our work. From my perspective, it was telling us that we were not spending time working together on systematic solutions. In an effort to learn more, I invited every one of our advocates to meet for coffee one-on-one. I recommended that the other directors on my team do the same thing to try and forge a different relationship. The advocates were going to have unique access to us, and as a result, we hoped to try to work proactively on behalf of students. Our message was that we wanted to invest our time more proactively and try to limit the time in reactive or individual mode.

We also decided, after hearing ideas from a few advocates during coffee, that we should begin a systematic advocate meeting. The messaging was the same: this would be a place for advocates to share themes or questions, as well as district staff to be able to share updates or requests. We planned to meet every six weeks and invited all advocates and all special education directors in our community.

It took us a few tries to get a cadence of how we were going to operate. We also noticed that we had several advocates who had no interest in working together in this way and were never going to join. That was okay, as our goal wasn't to get every advocate to the table; we could still accomplish our outcomes with whoever wanted to try this approach. After a few months, we got into the swing of things. At each meeting, our director team shared about district updates and work that we were doing, which allowed advocates to let parents know of changes or expectations. For example, we were updating our training around writing Prior Written Notice, and we were able to share our protocol. That allowed advocates to make requests of school teams when things weren't done correctly and for them to be able to say that they had seen the expectations and training firsthand. After convening for a few months, we began to hear a new theme—many advocates were asking about testing protocols around SLD. Why do we use this test for phonemic awareness and not that test? What is the process for observations to be documented? Is there a cut score or percentile score needed for a determination? It became clear that many of our costly Independent Educational Evaluation (IEE) requests were a by-product of this specific concern around testing protocols. Advocates were seeing different things from different schools and not getting their questions answered. Each SLD evaluation felt like a new experience that they had to interpret and understand. Parents did not feel that the process addressed their need to understand why their child was struggling at school. School staff were frustrated because they were always responding to questions in this area and spending a lot of time in multiple meetings.

At the next advocate meeting, we spent time asking what our advocates would like to see for a more consistent SLD evaluation protocol that went into the depth of information that would resolve these questions. They had recommendations of test names and templates they would want to see, and ultimately, they wanted more diagnostic data and more progress monitoring data to better understand how to write goals for a student.

As the power is in the process, we spent some time defining the problem and interviewing teachers and principals about this challenge. It felt big and impactful enough, and our target was both to have more in-depth information for the IEP process and also to reduce the amount of time we were all putting into getting questions answered. We spent the next six months bringing in groups of individuals to work on protocols for SLD evaluations. Once we had a good starting point, we brought it to other groups for their feedback. We learned that our SLPs had a real desire to dig into this work as it related to oral expression and listening comprehension, and we put together a subgroup to work on that strand of the protocols over the next three months.

We investigated a large variety of assessments and had a team make recommendations on some diagnostic tools that we wanted to adopt to align with the feedback of our advocate group. Then we brought back the work for our advocates to provide feedback on.

We were able to return to their original recommendations and answer why we were recommending one assessment over another. We had designed a set of supplemental assessments that could be checked out if we needed to dig deeper into any particular evaluation, an element that felt important to our advocate group, which sometimes has more specialized requests. We shared our observation protocols and spent time hearing feedback. The entire body of work took about nine months to complete, and our hope was to have this rolled out to all 375 special educators by late August to kick off the new year.

Everything came together as we coordinated the rollout plan. It was a lot of work to purchase materials, train staff on materials and help them understand why we made changes and what they were going to do to benefit them this school year. Most importantly, we shared why this was going to be great for students. By the following January, our advocate meetings continued; however, we had no IEE requests in the area of SLD and no more meeting discussion items in this area. By May of the same year, it was essentially radio silence from our community around SLD evaluations. We rarely heard a concern about these evaluations.

Community Leader Partnerships

The vision of our department includes developing community structures for our students. We want to see our students access jobs or college opportunities as meaningful members of our community. We had been developing job sites as a part of our Transitions Program, and one by one, we worked with employers in the community to find these opportunities. One by one, we were making great progress. At some point, we decided to leverage unexpected partners. We already had our internal partners identified, which included the School to Work Alliance Program, Transitions Leadership, principal of our Tech Program and more, but we were missing something. I began reaching out to other districts and just happened to get an email asking to take a meeting with a local businessman. I had one of my specialists meet with this person and found out that he had a lot of leadership in our community structures. He was on several boards and had time and energy to do some work. He wanted to help our students, and we were looking for help. The Transitions Program dean met with him a few times and taught him about the work we were already doing. He shared what his vision was and what he was hoping to accomplish.

After about a month, we realized that this was the type of partnership we were looking for. He was able to bring a completely new perspective. Whereas we were focused on what was within our capacity, he was focused on a community system that could expand our capacity. No money—he can help find some grants from the boards that he participates in. No time—no problem, he wants to offer his time. He was willing to be our voice and bring this work further than we could imagine. Together, we crafted a plan where he could spend a year working with local universities to create new pathways for our students and then work with his massive communities to advocate for inclusion in our workforce.

This work is still moving forward, and we are beginning to bring in other partners similar to this businessman and extend our work even more. We'll have to report out in a future edition of the book in regard to the detailed outcomes of this partnership, but for now, we will say there is significant promise in the work.

By working with community leaders and organizations such as our local dyslexia group or autism society, we can expand the work for our students. This has been a great way to integrate community needs into our schools, but it also promotes accurate and clear information about school systems that can be shared within our community. When was the last time you heard someone say something at school drop off, or at gymnastics or even leaning over the fencepost about a teacher or school event? Was that information accurate? Frequently, it is not; however, working with community leaders, we can get more accurate in what information is being shared between our families. This also can lead to leveraging community leaders who will surprise you with connections or resources that can be brought into the work of schools. Historically, we have seen community leaders frequently request changes to school systems—for example, a local Down Syndrome Association leader who is asking for a change in curriculum at a school. What we seek in partnerships is that these partnerships are reciprocal and can allow school systems to ask for assistance from our communities while also providing the assistance they need.

City Leader Partnerships

When we have updated our playgrounds at various schools, we have had principals bring in community representatives and business partners from their local area to provide feedback, in particular about the adaptive needs and the community accessibility. Together, we found creative solutions that our educators would not have thought of alone. At one school, we were designing a new playground and didn't have enough money to do what our community wanted. Welcome into our conversations community parks leaders who had an adjacent plot of land. They ended up creating a partner playground on their land to be able to meet all the needs of our groups between both spaces and have a real community space that extended beyond the school day.

Disability Group Partnerships

Another great school-based example can be found in the creation of parent groups. We have had many school-based leaders shy away from parent groups for parents of students on IEPs for all the reasons we shared earlier in this chapter. At one school, the special education leader decided to try these groups anyway despite his worries about conflict or failure. He began by inviting any interested parent, whether their child had an IEP or not. At first, there was a lot of information sharing that happened and over a few sessions, a theme began to emerge. His community was concerned about the messaging around autism at the school. Most of the representatives who were coming to the parent meetings were showing up in regard to this theme. The principal inquired with a variety of district-based individuals to learn more about how we could respond and what was already being done in this area. There were two camps of individuals in his parent group who wanted two very different approaches to our work with autism. The principal was ultimately able to bring in some adults with autism as unexpected partners who could share a viewpoint that wasn't as deeply embedded into our educational repertoire. These individuals spoke with his parent group and began to bring everyone together in a direction on behalf of his school. The parent group was able to impact how we offered training and messaging around neurodiversity and autism to their entire school community in a cohesive way as a result of this work. Together, they created whole school awareness protocols, developed resource banks of information and came together regarding approaches to April's autism awareness month on behalf of their unique community.

Nontraditional School Partnerships

In our current reality, we have many students with behavioral needs, and the threat assessment process is now a part of our national system. Historically, the school safety and special education leadership only got into the same room when there was a problem. We came from different theoretical backgrounds, different training and different goals for our work. This often meant that our problem-solving efforts, while well-intentioned, ultimately yielded opposing solutions. Special education leaders often felt that they were the only person in a room fighting for the student on an IEP while safety staff were fighting for the safety of the community.

As we continued to see more and more school threats, it became clear we needed time together to align and learn together. We already liked each other—that was never a problem—but we had to find some deeper alignment of effort. As simple as it sounds, we started by having each discipline do a presentation of the basic beliefs of their profession. We facilitated a series of weekly meetings where we discussed student scenarios and problem-solved in small groups that were multidisciplinary. By doing this, we had hashed out an aligned process or adjusted current processes often before we got into the room with any other staff. We were able to identify things that were not working, teach each other why we were advocating in the ways we were and begin a process of coming together. It was safe to explore hypothetical student threats before attempting to generalize to real scenarios. We found additional opportunities over two years to train each other's staff to better understand our work together. Training topics included special education law, understanding

IEPs, functions of behavior, understanding special education department make-up, special service providers and determining placement or least restrictive environment. As expected, we had many hard conversations, but both parties learned.

After two years of this work, one of the security directors came to me at a group event and was really excited about the training that he had done with his staff. They had spent time setting up expectations for the school year and discussing special education. They didn't need special education leaders to run this training because they knew the content and knew we were aligned. If that wasn't progress enough to note, he smiled from ear to ear and told me that the group had coined a new phrase. This year, they were going to be "sped-tacular" in their work.

We hope that with the stories in this chapter, you will begin to see the magic and deep value that including unexpected partnerships can bring to your work. By seeing the possibilities, it might be easier to move beyond the fear that this process will bring up for many leaders. Leaders also need to be aware that there will be hurdles. Time will be a hurdle, as we will always need more time to work in this way. Working through emotions and conflict will almost always be a hurdle when we bring individuals together who have much more varied viewpoints. Leaders of special education will need to thoughtfully consider which opportunities lend themselves to the inclusion of unexpected partnerships and which do not. By being thoughtful about selecting the right opportunities to invest in this way, we can remove the barriers of time. Most of the examples in this chapter could not have happened in one meeting or even one month. They took time. They took leaders who were thoughtful about crafting a process and hand selecting the partners to include.

When you begin to lead in this way, it is hard to ever think about working in another way again. You begin to realize that we no longer need to be fearful of the conflicts and challenges ahead of us in this special education leadership work because we always have the resources and experts within our schools and communities to help us find the solutions.

Closing Activity

Thinking about Unexpected Partners

When you run into an educational challenge, who are the partners you are most likely to seek out?

Who are unexpected partners specific to your community (Box 4.2) that might add to your list and offer new perspectives?

Can you think of any existing needs that you can involve unexpected partners in currently? If so, what areas and how can you start?

Notes

1 CAST, Inc. *About Universal Design for Learning*, Last modified 2023, Accessed on June 16, 2023, https://www.cast.org/impact/universal-design-for-learning-udl
2 Garmston, Robert J. and Wellman, Bruce M., *The Adaptive School*, Maryland, Rowman and Littlefield, 2016.
3 International Baccalaureate, *Our Mission*, Last modified June 6,2023, Accessed on June 16,2023, https://www.ibo.org/about-the-ib/mission/
4 Thinking Collaborative: Maximizing Capacity in Individuals and Organizations, *Cognitive Coaching Resources*, Last modified 2023, Accessed on June 16,2023, https://www.thinkingcollaborative.com/cc-resources

Reference

N., Sam, M.S., "First Impression," in *PsychologyDictionary.org*, May 11, 2013. https://psychologydictionary.org/first-impression/ (accessed June 16, 2023).

5

Modeling Collaboration

A Parallel Adult Learning Process

If we are going to implement collaborative problem-solving, we must model it and teach the process and benefits to our system. Readers who have bought into the benefits of collaboration are also presented with the challenge that helping others see and use this process is harder than it sounds. Imagine you are coming to an IEP meeting with an advocate who has been traditionally challenging, and you ask your team to come prepared to ask the advocate and family to start by proposing their best ideas for the student. To some, this could be career suicide—putting your team in a vulnerable place and not presenting yourselves as experts. How do we get others to see what we are now beginning to understand about collaborative partnerships? This chapter outlines that the teaching and learning process for adults is going to parallel that of the learning process we use with students. We have to model collaboration. We have to build capacity by showing success. We also may need to leverage leaders who have social capital to lead this work. Leaders have to collect artifacts, share their stories of success and failure and intentionally share the process of collaboration to grow the practice.

Have you ever heard the adage "be what you want to see" as a metaphor for successful parenting? The same holds true for educational leadership. As special education leaders, there is a parallel process between the learning and engagement we hope to achieve between ourselves and school staff, and that which we expect of with learning engagement between teachers and students. If we want the classroom to be full of unique learning experiences that meet the varying needs of our students, we also must create a similar experience for adults.

Most professional learning around classroom management or creating positive classroom climates involves making sure that students receive five, six or even eight instances of praise to one instance of correction. Research tells us that for learning, if we need to formally correct problem behavior, we must find at least four opportunities to highlight what a student is doing well.[1] This ratio applies not only to behavioral but also to academic learning and feedback. Picture reading a language arts essay with a dozen negative comments and no positive feedback. Students need to hear what they did well to be able to use the input on what they need to improve. Yet often, when observing a student with behavior barriers, we might hear a dozen or so corrections without instances of positive feedback. When we visit classrooms, we are keen on positive classroom climate benchmarks. For example, we look to make sure the norms or expectations are posted, that the students are called by their preferred name, that the teacher is offering more praise than correction and that the agenda and learning targets are posted.

In your experience with staff meetings, phone or in-person conversations with your supervisor, emails or professional development opportunities, do you experience the same? Does your team operate under a climate of five-to-one praise to correction? Does your yearly evaluation consist of mostly praise with a few areas of growth? When you go into a meeting, are you aware of the learning targets and objectives? Are there norms, expectations and a shared agenda? Do emails from your colleagues and supervisors mirror the considerations you might make if planning on having a difficult conversation with a student? Do you talk about strengths and possibilities going into a conflict with expectations of compromise?

This approach is what we are referring to as a parallel process. And this parallel process presents itself in unlimited iterations throughout our career. Perhaps you are leading a staff meeting on engaging diverse learners. Are you applying the strategies you are expecting the teachers to use in your meeting? It is so important that we "be what we want to see." Not only that, but by considering interactions as a parallel process, we are forced to include compassion, perspective taking and assume positive intent.

Let's think together about some of these parallel processes. How many of you have ever supervised recess? If so, you have invariably had kids approach you as the supervisor and share a situation where another student left them out, was not taking turns or wasn't playing fairly in a game of four square. Now, considering the parallel process, how often does a staff member drop by your office and share a situation among adult staff that has a similar theme? For example, a teacher shares that the other grade level teacher is not following through with agreements on learning targets, a teacher in a meeting is not sharing the air and dominates the work or a staff member shares that a teammate is not attending or showing up for work on time. When I ask you to think about variations of the parallel process, it won't be long before dozens of examples flood your memory.

> **BOX 5.1 Write down examples of parallel processes that you see in your special education leadership work.**

When you are considering how you might or have responded to these scenarios with adults, does it parallel with how you could coach or what you would expect of students? If you were to consider your expectation of staff interactions with families and students to how you interact with those you lead, what might you see? Are you pleased with your process being in alignment with your expectations of those you lead?

Moving back to the example of the child reporting that others are not taking turns or playing fairly on the playground. How would you expect those you lead to resolve that conflict? Should the staff expect the students to communicate with one another directly, should they solve it independently or do they need a facilitator to negotiate a compromise? When they do enter into a problem-solving conversation, how might the two students best communicate? Would they use "I" messages, state their feelings and identify a compromise? Now, apply this example to the adults you work with. Would or should you do the same with employee-to-employee conflicts? How can you guarantee that all of the expectations you would have around communication and problem-solving among students also exist for staff?

A few years back, a parent approached my supervisor with complaints specifically concerning my lack of understanding of their child's needs. This was a very complex situation in that, as a specialist, I was also charged with supporting the school team in designing services to meet the needs of this impacted student. The school staff believed that the student needed more support than they could offer. There were a variety of meetings and communications going on about this throughout the year. For the upcoming meeting, I was taxed with making the team, family, leaders and advocates reach some clarity of service. My intention was to both help the team be open and honest about the student's barriers and make sure the parent's wants and needs were heard and validated while at the same time understanding that the team needed to preserve the quality relationship they had formed with the family. The team needed to have a difficult conversation but served the student and family daily and wanted to preserve that rapport. I did my best to remain neutral during the meeting, but there were some difficulties in serving the student that the team needed assistance in voicing. The parent ultimately perceived the team's concerns as solely my professional opinion. The next step was an immediate communication from the parents to my supervisor. They expressed that everyone had been on the same page, except the specialist, which was me!

Upon receiving a phone call from the parent regarding their complaints about me, my supervisor reached out to discuss. As a leader, she was obligated to listen and validate any parent's concerns. As an employee, I was mortified. How could this situation that was carefully discussed and collaborative have gone so far off the tracks? Having my boss called feels like tattling and is counter to how any educator would like a parent to address a problem. I felt like my reputation was on the line, as I pride myself on being a connector in contentious meetings, bridging the gap between varied perspectives. I also know that in the chaos of the field of education, people don't generally call supervisors to offer instances of praise, only correction. My mind started spinning about the culture of tattling we sometimes have in our buildings. It's hard to be motivated to be diplomatic and engage in contentious meetings, knowing that the fallout could potentially be a complaint about you. Luckily, my supervisor also values the parallel process. She recognized in the situation that this was a very difficult meeting, and with the outcome being different than expected, the blame had been assigned to me. Not only that, but she allowed me an opportunity to continue to dialogue with the parent in a long-term effort to reclaim a norm of collaboration. I had to step outside of my comfort zone, but I generated a phone call to the parent, communicating that I understood they were dissatisfied with the meeting. I offered to be a listener and have a direct conversation with them. Unfortunately, the parent did not take me up on it, but it still had a positive outcome: in future meetings with them, there seemed to be an unstated compromise. I had owned, apologized and provided a platform to listen.

    It would have been so easy for my supervisor to just appease the complaint. I have had many supervisors in my career who would have immediately corrected me rather than sought to understand. However, recognizing that it's a parallel process between my supervisor and me, me and the parent/team and ultimately the school and the child, we chose to address the parent in a direct manner. This set a norm that we are all connected in our work with their child and all responsible for creating a climate of collaboration. We make attempts to understand each person's unique perspective through listening. This is the same parallel we use with students. We wouldn't just accept a complaint from one student on the playground. We would seek to understand, talk with both parties and then come together to find common ground. It might be appropriate for an apology or to share perspectives between students so that they don't have the same conflict over four square the next day.

This approach is going to be especially important for special education leaders who are shifting their practice to more collaborative approaches. If we tell our students to eat their vegetables but won't eat them ourselves, it usually doesn't work out very well. If we tell our staff to engage in collaborative approaches but we don't model them in our work, we can expect that collaboration won't go well. We build that capacity by showing successes from our work and then expecting that others will engage in similar ways.

Many years ago, our special education department was asked to host an advisory committee, mostly because there were so many complaints and concerns from staff at schools around the operation of special education. From that committee designed to advise on improvements in our districtwide operations, we created subcommittees. One of the most long-standing subcommittees has been our professional learning committee, a group typically composed of five to six individuals who will help create our districtwide special education professional learning days for each year. In our district, we bring together all 375 special education licensed staff for up to three half days a year for collective learning targets. This is one critical way that we can help special educators access the highly specialized content that they need to do their jobs. We've tried many iterations of this professional development plan with many varieties of failure. What we learned was that having a district representative create a multihour event that is supposed to target learning for that many individuals almost always doesn't work, especially when you put staff in a high school cafeteria on hard chairs with no coffee. Lessons learned. When this committee was formed, we had a few years of survey data and a list of requested learning topics, as well as feedback on what wasn't working. Staff wanted to have much more differentiation and much more time in small groups.

When we think of a parallel adult learning process, this applies immediately to this topic. Would we ever put all of our students in a lecture-style learning event for three hours in a cafeteria? Of course we wouldn't, and we shouldn't have done that with our adult learners.

Now you can see why we had to create an advisory committee. We needed a system for collaborating with educators to improve things. With all of the best intentions, leaders of special education need the input and creative collaboration of those doing the work every day. In the first years that this committee was created, we reviewed the survey data and began to plan for the following year's event. We decided that there was a benefit in everyone being together for a short period of time for a kickoff. We also decided that we needed a lot of time in differentiated groups and time actively engaging in content.

In order to model collaboration, we had our committee leaders begin the entire first session. They stood on a large stage and welcomed 375 staff into our comfy auditorium. They began the session by celebrating our collaboration to get to that day. They let everyone know that we had worked together in an advisory committee to make the day what staff members needed. They immediately got everyone up and moving in some icebreaker activities and modeled that this was going to be a different way of working.

We then moved to a keynote speaker who addressed legal topics, an area of strong interest from our survey results. The rest of the morning, we created conference-style breakout sessions based on topics of need. We set up various rooms related to addressing significant behavior. One room was specifically going to work with a teacher leader on trauma-informed behavioral approaches, while another was going to work on data-informed behavioral decision-making. Our teachers of autism programs worked together in another room on a virtual intervention platform, practicing how they would use this to support instruction. Yet another room was specific to preschool transition planning for preschool to kindergarten transitions. Another room had an expert from our IDA who would lead a hands-on session around teaching writing. We offered around 15 differentiated sessions that were aligned to survey results, brought in community leaders and teacher leaders to facilitate sessions and provided choice to most of our staff regarding what session to attend. We essentially had created a small batch, boutique-style learning opportunity.

After the first half day, we surveyed our educators again, as well as our presenters. The feedback was vastly different. Although there were a few negative notes (mostly about parking and space issues), the majority of the feedback was that staff simply wanted to participate in multiple sessions and didn't have the chance to enjoy all the great options offered.

After several years of working in this way, we also learned that we have to balance consistency with differentiation. What areas must we share information system-wide and consistently, and what information can be differentiated and targeted? For example, one year, we needed to re-norm our progress monitoring process, and it was clear we needed to do this work with all special educators for alignment. We were able to create a consistent lesson plan and then work in small groups to differentiate the content by job type. In other years, we can offer a variety of sessions on different topics, for example, trauma-informed behavior, where we can focus the content on a small group of interested staff and then offer that content to more groups over time as interest grows. As leaders, we have to constantly think about the requests and feedback of the teachers while also determining what level of consistency and universal messaging is needed.

Over time, this approach of working with a committee and offering differentiated, hands-on events became our working norm. Not only did it lead to better learning outcomes for our special education staff, but it also modeled the collaborative approach that we expect of our special educators. Now, when we come to IEP meetings where we are planning learning for our students, we don't want to see one teacher leading and doing the work. We expect the committee/team to come together and review the data and needs of the students and make collective decisions that result in better learning outcomes for our students. When we ask them to listen to the perspective of a private service provider who is at the IEP meeting, we have modeled that we also listen to perspectives as leaders and integrate those perspectives to the best of our ability in our plans.

One of the increasing themes that we highlighted in Chapter 1 is the theme of increased significant behaviors in our schools. This is another area in which we can model our collaborative approach for our staff and offer a parallel adult learning process. Oftentimes, schools are asked to involve a privately funded service provider in their work with students. We get frequent requests for BCBAs to come into schools to observe and collaborate, and often, they attend IEP meetings with families. As we see increased behaviors in schools, we want to shift our thinking from privately funded BCBAs as outsiders and instead begin working with them as collaborative problem-solvers. They observe home and clinic environments and have experiences that we don't have with the students. The same is true of our staff, who see students in different situations than a home-based provider does. When we have significant behaviors in schools, our students on IEPs often quickly get suspended or removed from their general education environments, where we might exacerbate the concern. Our hope is to have school-based staff work closely with the family and home-based BCBA to observe the student and find solutions. At our district office, we model that by bringing together our local BCBA community of providers and collaborating at a systematic level. When we began this work, we offered a round table discussion for our school-based BCBAs and home-based BCBAs to come together. Together, we were able to discuss how school-based BCBAs operated and why. We were also able to hear and respond to concerns within the community. We advertised these meetings in a way that our teachers at schools could see that we were modeling this work and engaging in collaborative relationships. By doing so, when we asked schools to do the same in the face of significant behavioral needs at their school, they knew that we had already set the groundwork to operate in this way. There were some unintended positive consequences that came from this process as well. By providing a platform of collaboration at a strategic level, we could form an overarching rapport with agencies and providers rather than getting stuck on specific student agendas. This rapport might last beyond the shared client services, laying the foundation for a more successful partnership with the next client.

Another lesson learned in working with the agencies through the BCBA roundtable was a lesson in social capital. By this, we mean starting with agencies that were most collaborative and highlighting that partnership. By design, we co-lead the roundtable work with those who were exemplary in partnering with our district initially. As others in the community saw that there were other BCBA agencies that were willing to work in this way, they were much more willing to do the same.

Similarly, our school-based leaders often need to figure out who has the social capital to make changes at the school. For example, if you are trying to implement a new writing intervention, but staff are resistant to the change, would you work with a quiet new teacher who might have been in conflict with your more veteran staff or would you have a greater impact with the veteran special education leader who can bring along the other staff?

Social capital is all about the networks that can be utilized to expedite the work. One of my favorite ongoing examples of this is within our autism principal leadership group. As autism began increasing exponentially at our schools, our district found more and more needs to create highly specialized autism programs in our inclusive school environments. As we opened new programs and developed our system capacity to support autistic students, often those with significant sensory and behavioral needs to regulate in a learning environment, we had a massive need to develop on-site special education leaders in the day-to-day work. We identified the problem and began to work on solutions. We set up a series of meetings and invited all of our principals of autism programs. We prepared shiny new agendas and content that was going to change their mindsets and improve operations immediately. We showed up to the meeting room, and only four out of our 15 principals were in attendance.

For about two years, we tried to motivate principals and help them understand that they needed this skill set, and we had the solutions with no real success. One principal even called and said that this was a group of 10 children in her school of over 1,000. She knew that this was important work; however, it was not something that she could invest this much time into.

A few years passed, and we were so proud of the work we were doing to develop these programs and yet our principal cohort was still not developing. It was at that time that one of our principal leaders reached out and asked if they could co-lead the work. This was a principal who others saw as a strong leader, one with a lot of social capital who could bring others along. They saw the value in it and had some ideas that could work. At the time, we were also getting pressure from executive leaders to limit our requests for principal time. So, we made both of these requests work and asked the principal leader if they would take on the lead for communication and gathering the group. We could manage logistics, and together, we could try another approach.

At the first meeting, only a few people showed up again, yet this time, the information came from the principal leader. This time, we went to a restaurant and met in a more comfortable space. This time, the principal leader spent a lot of time asking other leaders what they needed. Our district representative took notes and messaged the principal group afterward, noting that this principal was now leading the cohort and that we had outlined the work for the year with the list generated from their principal colleagues. At the next meeting, we had a slightly larger group. We also messaged that special education district leaders would begin to be present to hear from principals about their needs.

After two years of trying this approach, we showed up to one meeting, and four tables had to be put together at the restaurant. There were about 20 attendees, and we couldn't hear each other from one end of the table to another. The principals had been drawn in by their colleagues with social capital and were now more likely to attend. They continued to attend because they were able to problem-solve together and lead the work that they saw needed to be done. This group continues to this day, albeit with a newly appointed principal leader, and other groups have started to request to form using the same format.

These principals are now able to take that information back to their autism program classrooms. They can discuss how they have a cohort or professional learning community and model the way that their group operates. They can then expect parallel implementation of their autism program classrooms to create learning communities and collaborative structures between the teacher, paraeducators and service providers on behalf of their students.

So as you can see, our work is never-ending and is chock full of opportunities for both considering and demonstrating a positive parallel process. While we aren't always aware of these opportunities in the planning process, they present and re-represent themselves during most processes. Having the awareness that we are charged with "being what we want to see" can prompt us to recognize the parallels in any process. Developing a mechanism to check yourself on this is key to successful collaboration. Next time you are engaged in an adult scenario that feels contentious, pause to consider whether the answers or next steps might be best generated by imagining how we would teach students in a similar scenario.

Closing Activity

Modeling Collaboration

Where have you modeled collaboration for those that you lead? What do you hope your staff replicates from what you've modeled?

In what areas might you consider increasing your collaborative modeling?

Do these areas have parallel learning processes to what you expect from your staff?

Note

1 Piotrowski, Z., Erhart, A., Cidav, Z., et al. The Effects of Increasing Teachers' Praise-to-Behavior Correction Ratios on Disruptive Behaviors Among Students with Autism. *Penn LDI*. https://ldi.upenn.edu/wp-content/uploads/archive/The%20Effects%20of%20Increasing%20Teachers%20Praise%20to%20Behavior%20Correction%20Ratios%20on%20Disruptive%20Behaviors%20Among%20Students%20with-%20Autism_David%20Mandell.pdf

6

Empowering Others

How many of you grew up playing school? As a kid, this was the play theme that I chose the most. The first order of business was to designate who got to be the teacher. There could be only one, and that person was in charge, made all the decisions and was the authority in the game. The pupils were most definitely under the direction of this person. Fast-forward to your decision to work in education. When you visualized what teaching would be like, did you imagine a variation of playing school? Once you became a teacher, what informed your decision to then level up into leadership, administration, or a district specialist role?

Early in our careers, when our department was smaller, we were often charged with coming up with professional development opportunities. These were usually reactive in that a problem of practice had emerged at a building, and leadership had decided that a whole staff professional development was necessary to ensure growth. The charge was usually that we could offer training in order to develop the expertise necessary on-site. For example, IEP accommodations were not being implemented at a particular school, and we were asked to provide training to address the rules, requirements and implementations in this area to get them out of trouble.

I can remember in the early days doing a handful of staff professional developments on strategies for working with autistic students. I curated a list of my best practices—strategies that I knew worked because I had actually implemented them myself. I was determined to only deliver strategies that I personally knew and had had success with. When the staff training came, it was often me delivering my expertise to a group of teachers who had limited experience with the topic on which I was presenting. A lot of learning occurred. It was not unusual to receive glowing feedback from participants. I felt confident about my public speaking skills and was apprehensive about schools having anyone but our department presenting on topics of expertise. If given a choice, our department would present to ensure that best practice in the content area was covered. We usually declined outside third-party professional development because of cost and, frankly, because we would need to broker the content to ensure quality. It was frankly scary to think of someone downloading our staff content that might be incongruent with what we wanted them to receive.

This resistance to collaboration with outside third parties was reinforced in the few times that schools had unilaterally contracted with someone outside who had introduced strategies that were counter to our vision. Often, after having site-based presentations, we would begin to hear reports of the content presented and immediately become concerned about what we might have to redo in order to get things back on track. On one occasion, a school contracted an outside clinician to come speak on trauma-informed practices. While trauma-informed practices are a definite must, this person did not provide a balanced perspective and not only shared their strategies but went into great detail about how some other common and evidence-based practices used by practitioners throughout our district were contraindicated and should not be used in schools. This was concerning in that the whole staff had received training to the contrary of what she was presenting only weeks before. Staff were left puzzled and unsure of how to proceed, echoing that they had been given two opposing pieces of guidance. After the presentation, I was charged with meeting with the presenter to help with alignment, and we engaged in an effort to discuss our content, her content and how they may overlap rather than diverge. This meeting, while emotionally charged, yielded a shared product that encompassed both of our agendas and didn't need to discard one approach at the expense of another. Having to solve this collaboratively was a valuable lesson learned, but it felt reactive and exhausting.

Fast-forward five years to a time when our practice, vision and mission were well established within the district. We had extensive professional learning available for the critical mass of educators in our district on the prioritized topics. We had extensive coursework available in the area of autism, reinforcement systems and schedules, restraint and seclusion, executive functioning, literacy interventions and so forth. When possible, we were meeting with presenters to ensure alignment, but not consistently and only when asked. However, now the challenge had become that our requests for professional development were starting to exceed our capacity to fill the requests. Additionally, we were having to divide and conquer but weren't sure that all of our district leaders were sending a consistent message. Out of necessity, we needed to come up with a proactive way to expand our offering while keeping the high standards for best practices that we had established.

Around that time, our specialists attended Adaptive Schools training.[1] We began to learn not only about the power of collaborative thinking but also some protocols for facilitating this type of collective learning. As we grew in our collaborative understanding, we made the departmental shift to a new and different approach to planning professional development. Rather than putting out fires after a learning event went astray, we decided to be proactive and collaborate on the front end of the work, focusing more on empowering others in the process. In response to outside trainers coming into our schools, we started asking for a preplanning meeting in which we could review the proposed content to look for any land mines. With that in mind and after a collaborative review and discussion, the third party would be prepared to deliver a quality professional development experience. They felt successful as they were prepared for the environment and context that they were coming into for the learning, and we felt successful because we could plan for alignment. On occasions, presenters were even observed to repeat some of our engaging activities with other audiences. There was a mutual benefit to working in this way, and the presenters were empowered to lead the work, knowing we were aligned.

We also decided to tackle the concerns of common messaging from our internal department. One of the systematic ways that we ensured that our practice would continue despite educators coming and going from our team was to develop a rubric (Table 6.1) of our norms and agreements for outside presenters (the same

TABLE 6.1 Required Quality Professional Development Rubric

	Item Completed	*Reflections*
Start on time, end on time		
Agenda is posted (e.g., slide deck, on a wall)		
Greet, introductory or grounding activity to activate learning		
Participants are given access to all materials and/or PowerPoints before or during training		
Two to three activities per hour, no more than 10–12 minutes of a lecture at a time, including individual and whole-group activities		
Slides have the Boulder Valley School District logo, bullets, visual images, color are spell-checked, formatted with consistent font and proofread for spelling and grammar		
Multiple modes of learning (visual, auditory, kinesthetic) are present. Add captioning during virtual learning and record		
Participants are provided with a feedback rubric after the event		
Training has SMART (specific, measurable, attainable, relevant and time-bound) goals and objectives		
Preplan with stakeholders if appropriate		
Additional Optional Quality Components		
Manage time (preplan and practice ahead to make sure you get to all content)		
Offer breaks		
Goals and objectives are linked to teacher/paraeducator effectiveness standards		
Test technology before and work with porter for room arrangement		

norms we set for our internally provided events.) Through our rubric, we were able to leave these planning meetings with the trust that the learning event would be engaging and collaborative and highlight best practices. It is important to note that this rubric was established using a consensus protocol. Our leadership suggested norms independently, then grouped themes and then participated in discussions about which aspects should be required or suggested. Pro tip: if you replicate this rubric with your professional development, remember the power is in the process! Use this as a guide and enrich it by having your staff generate their own.

We noted earlier that our other challenge was receiving more requests for professional learning than our department had the capacity to offer. In response to this and with our newfound learning through collaboration, our district began to shift professional development to a mostly collaborative or co-teaching model. Any time we received a request to lead a site-based professional development, we began asking for a building-based staff partner to share in delivery. This had so many unintended positive outcomes. Do you remember the learning activity compared to retention of knowledge chart (Table 2.1)? People learn best by teaching, which meant that having a staff member share the delivery ensured that this person had built more expertise than others in their building. Essentially, we were leaving behind a site-based expert. We know that being able to program for generalization is one of the most important elements of learning. Also, having a site-based co-teacher would allow for instant buy-in with the staff, as their trusted colleague was presenting. It increased engagement and energy and empowered schools to own the learning and continue their growth in that area.

At one high school, we were asked to provide a one-hour learning session around accommodations. As soon as we received the request, we asked for a meeting with the special education teachers and administrators who are on-site every day. We asked what they saw as the core concerns and heard a lot of reasons why this was necessary content for their staff. We then asked if they would be willing to co-teach the content with district leaders or even take the leap to lead the content themselves with our support. It felt clear that their colleagues had known about accommodations, and they knew they were supposed to implement them if they were in an IEP. They were going to perceive even the very best one-hour, district-led event as something else they needed to sit through. We wanted them to engage in professional learning and actually learn. A year before, we would have been perfectly happy to provide that one-hour event and know that people would learn something. Now that we knew that we could work collaboratively and empower others on-site to achieve better outcomes, we had to take that approach. With a little nudging, the school staff decided to lead the event and asked that a district leader attend to show the importance of the work. They began planning, and we met for a second discussion. It was now our role to coach them through the event—how could you get to engaging activities quicker in your agenda? Do participants understand why they are learning this content and how it is relevant to them? What stories can we share that would make this more meaningful? After the second session, the assistant principal asked if we could extend this to a series. If we had just a one-time event, they realized that accountability was going to be a challenge. With permission, we then began planning a four-event series that included reviewing IEPs and 504s of their own students, department discussions of implementation in each content area and simulations of what it feels like to be a student with a disability who has no accommodations. All of this occurred as co-taught sessions led by school-based staff with resources and co-planning supported by our district team.

BOX 6.1 Empowering Others' Approaches

- Identify each staff member's existing area/s of expertise
- Identify each staff member's desired area of expertise
- Identify site-based leaders (official and unofficial)
- Develop professional development norms and expectations
- Co-deliver content, skilling up leaders
- Program for generalization and expanding building capacity

Another empowering and far-reaching approach to professional learning that we often take includes curating post-session experts on-site. This is done by completing the learning event and then developing a list of examples or experts on-site that can provide ongoing expertise. In one example, we implemented an extensive classroom management and behavior series at an elementary school. This was a two-day event that taught and practiced at least 15 explicit behavioral strategies for preventing and responding to behavior. Within the training, participants got an opportunity to role-play, script and practice each strategy with a partner. As a follow-up, we scheduled time in each participant's classroom to observe implementation. We did a 15-minute observation in order to see the strategies at play. After observing, we were able to curate a list of who in the building had each strategy or skill acquired. With permission, we were able to make a building-wide list of one person who could be contacted in-house for guidance on each of the skills. This would have never been possible without taking a collaborative approach to the delivery of the content. The staff on the building list were empowered as school-based experts in the content area, allowing future opportunities for learning and growth.

Now, we can proudly say that collaboration in professional development design and implementation is the norm in our district Special Education Department, even seeing elements of our work being adopted now in other departments. Most recently, we had a team of 12 site-based service providers develop and film our district paraeducator training series. Each module is delivered by two site-based providers in an asynchronous format, and the group of 12 providers owns the content rather than one person. Paraeducators are now able to have content delivered by people that they encounter in their daily work versus unknown specialists. By having 12 masters of content versus one, we have been able to further expand the capacity of those presenters and the reach of professional development exponentially.

What we learned by releasing control in work such as professional learning was that, by empowering others, the work not only expanded exponentially, but it also released us from extreme amounts of pressure. Previously, every decision was ours to own, and when something didn't go well, it was completely on our team to own and respond. As we shifted to collaborative models, we found a great amount of freedom in being a part of the process and not the sole leader of the process. By empowering others and working collaboratively, we get to begin a process of letting go. Leaders instead focus on curating the opportunities or questions and are charged with listening and facilitating rather than always making the decision. If you work in a system that isn't very collaborative, you might feel as if you are the solution. It's your job to solve the problem or show up with the answer. In the mindset shift presented here, we have begun to learn that there is a much further reaching impact when we empower others. In the previous example, we could have had one person create the classes and had some great learning. Typically, those courses would see a handful of participants and good learning would happen. Instead, we had 12 leaders who all found deeper learning in the process and then were able to promote the courses and provide deeper learning at 12 sites. By empowering these leaders, we shifted from impacting a school or small group to reaching hundreds of teachers at the schools of these 12 individuals.

> "Successful leaders understand that true power comes not from exercising control, but from empowering others."
> Jesse Lyn Stoner, founder of Seapoint Center for Collaborative Leadership

Just as professional learning is a need found in every district, partnership with principal leaders is common in every school system that we have experienced. Empowering principals is one of our most important roles as district special education leaders. Most district leaders of special education have several principals that they work with. We work in a district of 30,000 students and a 12 percent population of students on IEPs. In total, we have around 54 principals and a variety of assistant principals who lead special education practices on their school site. In a district our size, the day-to-day questions and scenarios that pop up are mostly addressed through school-based leadership. Our district leaders spend a good portion of the week on calls with school-based leaders, working through scenarios and helping to ensure appropriate practices and responses are in place.

One particular school year, on the first day of school, we received a usual first-day phone call from a new principal. This principal had been an assistant principal for a few years prior and had been newly hired to lead an elementary school. She was calling to let us know that she had just suspended an autistic kindergarten student for hitting. Okay, not how we wanted to start off our work together. We talked with the principal and eventually with the parent, who was as quick to call us with a complaint. The parent had immediately lost trust with the school and principal, and we spent a few weeks sorting out a request for the child to be moved to another local school. Now, in prior practice, this would have been a blame game scenario where the principal would have been called in and told that they had done wrong. The whole thing just didn't go well. Did anyone know about this student's behavior plan? Were we implementing the student plan in those first hours of school? Did we work together on a transition to school for this student who struggled with transitions? How did we set up classroom routines? Why did the student hit another student? There were just so many questions. And yet, scenarios like this happen all the time. We can blame and shame each other, or we can use this as a learning opportunity.

We decided to make sure that this was a learning opportunity and begin empowering the principal in how to better process through questions and scenarios for students on IEPs. We realized quickly that she hadn't had to do much of this in her prior role, and this would be a learning curve—but a learning curve for us together. Everyone had ownership in the problem, and everyone had ownership in the solution. It was as much our fault for our system not preparing this principal as it was hers for the impulsive response.

This principal also had an intensive autism program on-site, which gave us a lot of opportunities to work together. We exchanged cell phone numbers and asked if we could spend more time on-site working together. Over the course of about two years, we spoke at least weekly to problem-solve something.

How can we problem-solve this teacher's scheduling concern? How can we respond to the parent's email? What can we do for this student who isn't making any progress? The message we were constantly sharing in many different ways was that we are a team in leading special education. That principal no longer had to worry about a response to a family being "wrong," and we no longer had to worry about needing to have all the answers because we became a collaborative partnership to lead special education at the school.

As a part of this work, we naturally attended lots of IEP meetings together. At the start, as district leaders, we modeled how we would run the meeting. Often, the meetings had points of contention, and we modeled how to listen and really seek to understand the parent's point of view before responding. We modeled how to include a general education teacher in the IEP process and how to stop a meeting when we truly didn't have an answer and needed some time to problem-solve for a successful solution. We modeled our vision for supporting students with IEPs in every interaction and meeting. Let's face it: this is nuanced work and requires coaching and modeling for principals.

Within two years, we began fading back our support. At first, it was intentional: we would go to an IEP meeting and ask the principal or teacher to take the lead. "Today, I'll just be the notetaker if that's okay." Little by little, there were fewer phone calls and emails and less need for our district staff to come to meetings. Parents started calling our offices with appreciation for the principal who had unique care and understanding for our students with disabilities. They noted that they had never seen a principal who knew the special education laws and spent so much time listening.

The shift was palpable. After a few short years, that principal went on to be a principal at one of our largest schools, with several assistant principals working for her. As is often the case, the assistant principal at this larger school took the lead in special education and was now under the leadership of this principal. Our district team began the same process with this assistant principal with similar results. What was different now was that their principal had had so much collaboration in developing their vision and approach to special education leadership that she could support the assistant principal in complete alignment with the district leaders.

One day, we visited the school to work with the assistant principal on a behavior challenge, and the principal quietly asked us to come meet with her in her office. She said that she didn't want everyone to know we were talking because she empowered her assistant principal to do the work of leading special education. She said that she noticed that accommodations were not being implemented at her school and that staff did not seem to understand the difference between accommodations and modifications- and asked if we noticed the same. Yes, absolutely 100 percent correct. She said that this was a core equity concern that needed to be addressed and that she would empower the assistant principal to work with our department and put together a plan. If you read the earlier parts of this chapter, you know how that process went from there to create the professional learning activities.

With a quick two-minute conversation, it was clear that all that collaborative learning was a core part of who this principal was as a leader and that she was now empowering her leaders in that same vision.

This type of work happened over and over again at this school. From the collaboration with this one leader who was empowered to lead a common vision for students with disabilities, we collectively began to empower other leaders at this new school.

This principal ultimately took an executive leadership position in our district. Within her very first week, special education had a seat at the table with this leader. We were invited to interviews for high-level positions. We were brought into conversations with other principals. Our students with disabilities were in the everyday planning and thinking of this leader, in great part because of our long-term collaborative approach. We had empowered this leader of special education from a small school to a bigger school to district-wide impacts, and her beliefs that had been cultivated in that process were a part of her leadership identity. Students with disabilities were not an afterthought; they had to be a part of every element of our organizational planning. Empowering this one leader had an impact so much wider than we could have ever imagined on that first day when the kindergartener was suspended.

We see this time and time again with the approach to collaborative special education leadership between district leaders and principals. Over and over, principals move to new districts or new leadership positions, and they carry this learning with them. We've had many colleagues become superintendents and move to leadership roles in districts across the country. Repeatedly, they call us for guidance or discussion because they learned the value of this way of working. They know we don't always have the answer, but together, we can collaborate on how to begin finding solutions.

This approach has a lot of unintended positive consequences. First, it reduces the time needed by district special education leaders to respond to a particular school. Whereas there is a huge time investment early on, there is a long-term positive impact as that leader fades back their need for district support. Systemic solutions that save us time are definitely needed in our underfunded area of work. Maybe more importantly, this approach also gives the school and the school-based leader the opportunity to have the knowledge and skills to make decisions on their own.

We have one colleague who was a principal with us for at least ten years who used to call us and say, "Give me the tools." They wanted someone to process and plan with them and then let them lead the work. They didn't want to have to call in a special education director to manage a difficult meeting. They believed that when we did that, it only served to give a family the message that they needed to go to "the district" to get anything done. Instead, he would say, "Give me the tools," and we would spend an hour on the phone talking through scenarios. Parents are asking about this kind of service—here's how you can respond. My teacher is really upset, and I need to help her voice some things at the meeting. How can we do that? What if we disagree? What if we need a break? We talked through the "ifs" and the "whys" and gave him the tools. He often just needed a conversational model to make sure his thinking was on track, and then he felt confident delivering the message.

Another principal recently texted and asked if she really could lead a meeting involving a very upset teacher. She was questioning her ability to manage a unique conflict. I texted her back and said, "We aren't available at that time tomorrow; however, you are basically a special education director after all our work together. I know you can do this; let's talk it through tonight." She called laughing, telling us her strategy for the meeting and that she knew she would just stop the meeting if she couldn't handle it. I gave her a few notes and suggestions, and she was once again confident in how to proceed. Within 24 hours, she had messaged back that the meeting went beyond great and that she (jokingly) believed she earned her special education license because she had been so empowered to lead in this area time and time again.

Another impact of this approach is that it provides the relationships and safety for school-based leaders to make mistakes as they learn. Imagine if we had responded to that first-time principal and told her how wrong she was in making that suspension decision. That might have broken relationships and trust or caused them to feel unsafe in making future decisions. Instead, we put in place high levels of support and collaborative learning that build a safety net. The principal knew that we would be there together when things didn't go well. And there were many times things didn't go well!

Co-teaching for professional learning and co-leading special education with our principals at our schools are both all about empowering others. We must "sneak in" extended outcomes of the work, much as the proverbial sneaking in of vegetables into the kids' meals. Our mindset changes and extensions of deep learning are mashed up into the pasta sauce so that they are imperceptible at the onset. We design, curate and facilitate and can let go of the terrifying need to have all the answers. Brave special education leaders can free themselves from some of the burden of leadership by empowering others and developing their skills in collaboration.

Closing Activity

Give It a Try

What is your worst fear about trying a collaborative approach to special education leadership?

What is one step you can take to empower others in your work?

Who would be a list of stakeholders who could benefit from this approach?

Note

1 Garmston, Robert J. and Wellman, Bruce M., *The Adaptive School*, Maryland, Rowman and Littlefield, 2016, From Thinking Collaborative LLC out of Highlands Ranch, Colorado. https://www-origin.abebooks.com/servlet/BookDetailsPL?bi=31589587540&searchurl=an%3Dgarmston%2Bco%2Bdeveloper%2Bcognitive%2Bcoaching%2Badaptive%26ds%3D10%26sortby%3D17&cm_sp=msrp-_-msrpdesc-_-bdp

7

Strength of Students

Students are at the center of everything we do as special education leaders, and therefore, we think they deserve their very own chapter.

So often, there is a disconnect between the experience that a student is having and the experience that the staff thinks the student is having. Having two daughters in middle school, I experience this regularly. I have a positive perspective of their school's inclusivity, a school with a climate of students recognizing one another's strengths and significant efforts in the area of equity and inclusion. I have the unique opportunity to visit their school often to work alongside the adults in the building and feel confident that this culture exists and that teachers implement acceptance. I see it firsthand. Yet, frequently on our drive home from school, where we debrief the day, I get stories of inequity, stories of kids actively or passively being excluded. How can there be such an incongruence between the experience we think we are providing and the experience that students might be receiving?

One of the most important collaborators in our work to redesign special education is the very students that we aim to serve. Despite our best efforts, we have a history in special education of not accounting for the actual experiences and desires of our students, as noted in the previous paragraphs. We have a system that is set up to create goals FOR students, to design lessons FOR students, with data collected ABOUT students and most often, we have a system that has the student as the recipient of all this effort with only a high-level road map of where we might be going together. If we are going to do better and see different results, then we need to include students as collaborators and partners each step along the way.

This chapter looks at two different ways to view this need. First, we explore how we can collaborate and better understand student strengths as special education leaders responding to requests of unmet needs. As responders, we are called in when there is a problem of some sort, and we are asked to find a solution or act as gatekeepers to the next step. This happens to principals and district leaders every day, and we can improve outcomes by using a process that starts with an early understanding of student strengths. Second, we look at how we can partner with students more directly in designing their learning, as well as in peer support processes. We can close this perception gap between students and educators if we work more closely with students and view them as resources in their own learning environments.

Using Student Strengths for Responder Success

Working in the field of autism, understanding student strengths is paramount to motivation and engagement. If we do not have a firm understanding of autistic student's preferences and desires with the willingness to embed those into content, we are bound to fail. Although this may be true for any learner, it is especially true with those who are neurodivergent to "ensure that differences are not viewed as deficits" (Baumer, 2021). How can we invest the time to really understand their restricted interests, foster those interests and desires and build on those strengths? The field of autism has a history of trying to block or change restricted interests and a desire to normalize autistic individuals. It's counterintuitive to enhance or strengthen the very thing that appears to be getting in the way of learning. If we can authentically and collaboratively work alongside autistic individuals and build upon their strengths and goals, the results can far exceed our previous expectations.

A recent example of this comes to mind, although this same example has presented itself in countless iterations in my professional career. It might vary, but it is always the same. I walk into a class, and the class is receiving whole group instruction, often in the middle of a writing task. The student I am there to observe, a student with a disability, is in the back of the room, looking out the window, examining some items, maybe even playing with or even destroying materials they have acquired. The staff relay that the student refuses to engage in writing, and they are not sure of the student's present skill level because they bypass the output part of learning (e.g., they refuse to write). I glance down; the student has a flexible shark in his hand. I ask him the names of three sharks; he shares three names with ease, along with his favorite kind of dinosaur. Meanwhile, the class is studying the letter U. They learned that U is for umbrella and U is for ukulele. The student doesn't care about umbrellas and ukuleles. With a quick Google search on the phone in my pocket, I find dinosaur names beginning with the letter "U." I write the word Udanoceratops. I locate and write it on a whiteboard and ask the student to underline the U. He immediately engages. I look for a few more dinosaur names that have the letter U; he underlines. I then reassess what it is that the class is doing. They are tracing and practicing writing the letter U. I write ten dotted U's on the whiteboard; he traces them. I draw a checkbox and give written directions to the student to write five U's. He does. Staff remarks, "We didn't know he could read or write." Finding out the student's strengths and differentiating the task to connect to those strengths and interests allowed him to be meaningfully included in the task. More often than not, adjusting tasks in alignment with such strengths allows the adults to see that the student is more capable than ever expected. By using the concepts of priming and behavior momentum as described, the student is able to access instruction.

I know what you're thinking: we don't have the staff to do that. That sounds nice, but we don't always have the resources to do that! What if we were to consider the strengths of our students in finding a solution? You might be hard-pressed to find a classroom that didn't have a learner who was gifted and talented and needed an extension to their learning. By considering the strengths of all learners in the community, we might be able to find a learner who could do exactly what I did on the whiteboard and generate not only their own learning but also the learning of the autistic student. Most students are more responsive to a peer accommodating their learning than adults anyway. It's a win-win situation.

Have you had similar calls for help as a leader? Are there times when you arrive at a class as the requested person to intervene with a student demonstrating significant behavior? If you have, you probably share with me the understanding that no matter how skilled you are, you might not have instructional control with this learner and also feel familiar with the pressure to find a viable solution. If you are not successful, the staff's thoughts that this learner should not be in their environment will be reinforced. If the teacher hasn't been successful, and I can't come in and show them differently, then it must be impossible for this student to learn in this environment, right? This happens to special education leaders time and time again, which can make it feel like a setup being a responder.

This brings us to our first rule of being a responder. We ask that everyone begin with a strengths-based mindset and an open mind that the student with the need can in fact learn and that the outcome might be positive. We are showing up with the focus of supporting success and taking all possible steps toward the student learning and growing in their current environment. Often, even before we arrive in a classroom, we are presented with an educator who mentions that they know that the student cannot learn or cannot learn in this environment and that we are the next step toward getting them out of their classroom. If that is the basis for the request, we have to have a hard conversation even before we walk into the classroom. We make it clear that the context for our work is collaborative, that it is our goal to find how the student can learn and that it is our expectation that all students will learn. We have to start the process from this mindset of strength and also set the tone that learning happens in small steps rather than giant leaps. This is critical contextual work that helps to manage expectations and set the tone even before stepping into the classroom.

Next, when we are ready to step into the classroom, we start with some strength-based questions to set everyone up for success. Knowing what motivates the learner you are supporting is the best way to enter the room. Before we even begin an observation or consult, my questions are usually as follows in this order:

- What does the student want?
- What are they looking forward to today?
- What is the task at hand, or what were you trying to get them to do?
- What excites or interests the student in general?
- What is their greatest strength in general?

Once I know these things, I can effectively formulate a plan to assist. I will preface my description of generating a response with the requirement that I must partner with a present staff member in being the responder. It's going to be a WE approach, a rule that has become my non-negotiable. After hearing the answer to the questions, I do a few additional inquiries or actions in order to allow me to quickly sort an effective response, always keeping in mind the four functions of behavior[1]—attention, access to preferred items/tasks/activities, escape/avoid demands, and automatic reinforcement. I then ask the following in an effort to illuminate the correct targeted goal:

- If the student were to demonstrate a skill or communication right now, what would it be (i.e., following directions, waiting, making a request for an item)?

Depending on the response, we will collaboratively discuss these more focused questions that lead to potential strategies that we will try during our time together:

Question to Consider	Likely Function	In the Moment	Strength-Based Strategies
Would this be happening if the student was alone? Would this be happening to this intensity if there were fewer/no people? How can I attach my attention to an approximation of what I want to see?	Attention Maintained	Decrease adult responders or other students' presence. Provide opportunities for student to have privacy. Identify and praise approximations.	Scheduled time to talk with teacher about topic of interest Drive-by praise—have each member of student's school team randomly drop into class and provide attention two times per day Make me an expert—tell the student the agenda for the lesson and program a chance for them to be the one to correctly answer when the question is asked
Was the student transitioning out of a preferred task or told no?	Access (to preferred items, task, activity) Maintained	Remind the student of the next opportunity for that activity. Prompt requests to ask for another minute. Prompt functional communication "I want."	Take students special interest and embed it into curriculum and tasks Build and practice transition routines Teach procedure for requesting more time
Was the student being asked to do an academic demand? If there was not a work demand or direction would this be happening? If I said, "You don't have to do x," would this stop? If I started the task or helped, would things de-escalate?	Escape or avoid task or demand	Determine when student was last having success and rewind to that moment. Task analyze the first small approximation of the task that the student is likely to be successful at (i.e., sharpen your pencil and open your book). Prompt using words to ask for help or break.	Provide opportunities for accommodations like scribe or technology Provide alternative tasks that are aligned with students present levels or interests Embed preferred items, tasks, and activities into steps of task Know preferences and alternate preferred and nonpreferred tasks

We use these frames and have a discussion about which approach best fits the unmet need in the classroom. We formulate an action plan with the on-site partner and a timeline to follow up. This leads to another rule—always create a plan for monitoring to determine if the action plan is working. Often, I will leave and send an email summarizing the discussion, time line for checking back in and what we agreed to as an action plan.

> **BOX 7.1   Responder Rules**
>
> - Begin with a strengths-based mindset—learning can happen and starts with small steps
> - The WE approach—always partner with a current on-site staff member
> - Motivators first—ask questions to understand student strengths and interests at the onset
> - Functions—keep in mind functions of behavior when creating a response plan
> - Monitoring- create a plan for monitoring if the plan is working

The Strengths of Students as a Classroom Resource

At a time when hiring and retaining high-quality staff is a challenge (see Chapter 8), one of the most underutilized strengths in our school buildings is that of our students. Students are our future educators, and by viewing them as one of our best resources in a school building, we are also helping to create interest and excitement that ultimately draws people in to become educators.

Maybe even more importantly, students are more creative educators than adults are. If you ask an adult to solve a math problem, they most often will show you the way they learned and have a hard time giving you alternative approaches. If you ask a student, they will surprise you by giving multiple approaches, stories and examples. If you ask my daughter who taught her math class last year, she will say the student next to her. Their creativity, innovation and energy are incredible strengths that can benefit all classrooms.

The easiest way to integrate student strengths in innovating special education is by developing a process to include students in their own IEP processes. Even a first grader can answer some questions and provide input about their favorite things (interests), what they are good at (strengths) and what they want to accomplish this school year (goals.) Students of all ages can give input to make their IEPs more meaningful. This conceptual model can be extended even more as we develop goal-tracking systems that students are a part of.

I recently worked with a preschooler who had speech goals. The preschooler was able to tell us that they love balloons, that they really want to carry a backpack this year and that they are really good at dancing. All of those tidbits made their way into the IEP plan. They were really struggling with one of the articulation goals, and the IEP team discussed how we could use the student input to make this more motivating. Together, we set up a system where they had a sheet of paper that they colored in every time they worked on their speech goal. That sheet went home in the backpack that they were proud of, and they had the responsibility of showing their parents the sheet. The parent was then able to buy some balloons, which were a reward for any time five sessions were completed. Very quickly, the student became excited about participating in speech lessons, and they earned several balloon rewards. Midyear, the data sheet became a graph of the progress they were making so that they could actually engage in understanding that their speech percentages were improving. The student was not simply given a goal, and the data was not collected on the student; instead, the entire process was collaborative, and progress was elevated as a result. Even at a preschool level, kids are motivated by their strengths and can have meaningful involvement in their own progress.

By fourth and fifth grades, I've had students helping to monitor their own goals more actively and creating plans to exit special education. I had a fourth grader come to me when I was teaching, and he asked how he could get out of this "stupid class." We sat down and talked about his IEP and discussed what goals were on it. I was surprised to realize he had no idea what his own plan involved. We discussed that the way to be able to remain in his general education classes all day would be for him to meet his goals and gain the skills to do so. In his case, his goals were both academic and behavioral, and this was going to be a lot of work. He was really motivated and interested, and I asked what he needed to be able to take some steps toward this goal. We collaboratively decided that he needed to be a part of tracking his goals so that he could be aware of when he was on target or not. He also wanted to be a part of the next meeting to discuss his interests. It took a few years for him to finally get to a place where he made enough progress to remain in general education classes all day, still with some special education support at times. However, this new path was now defined and aimed in the direction that he wanted to take. It wasn't just the adults leading him forward toward some unknown goal. He was aware of the work he needed to do, and he was helping his team be aware of what he wanted and why. When he refused to engage in a task or had challenging behavior, he could now see how it impacted his goal progress because he was a part of monitoring that information.

As students get older, the collaborative IEP process just continues to grow in depth and intensity. By the time students are in high school, many can help lead their IEP. The student-led IEP process[2] allows students to take an active role in planning for and developing their own IEP. This is a critical step in helping them learn self-determination as well as growing their own awareness around their self-advocacy. They ultimately will leave the education system and will need to know what they need and how to advocate for it. There is no better way to teach those abilities than through their own IEP process. Unfortunately, even in our own district, we don't see student-led IEPs happening very much. This may be in part due to the need for teachers to teach students how to engage effectively in this process and the many time constraints on our teachers. It's an area we know we need to grow.

When we have observed students leading or even partially leading their IEP, the results are incredible. Recently, I participated in a meeting with a student who had really struggled their entire school career. They had been in and out of mental health treatment centers and really struggled with basic executive functioning or responding to any request from an adult. Yet, the student was highly gifted, very verbally expessive and had a very clear goal for their life after high school. The adults working with the student all had very clear opinions of what they wanted for the student. The parent wanted him to attend school beyond age 18 because he had so many more skills to work on. The educators all had concerns about him attending school past age 18 because the social dynamic of him remaining after all of his friends and peers had graduated was only going to exacerbate his inability to make progress. As a special education leader working on his plan, I asked everyone to let us use the process and to engage the student to lead or co-lead the plan.

This didn't start off well, as we all logged into the virtual meeting and realized that the student wasn't at home and wasn't at school. After about 15 minutes, the student was found, and we had a quick conversation about not wandering around the school building before we began the meeting. From there, we introduced the IEP process and asked the student to lead the discussion. He shared that he had been talking with his teachers and couldn't really come up with a plan that he could engage in the following school year. He wanted to learn some skills, but he also knew that he was fairly stubborn and was only going to come to school if it meant something to him. We offered options—partial day with a job for credit in the afternoon, concurrent enrollment in a local community college and an option to graduate. We asked the student what goals he wanted to work on and asked each other member of the team to share anything else they wanted him to know as we made a plan. The student asked to take a night or two to think about the discussion and then to come back together.

Ultimately, the parent came to realize that we were not going to get anywhere by forcing the student to come to school if they were not invested in the plan. The school staff realized that there was much that we could do for the student if they were invested in a plan. Everyone was open to following the student's lead, as that would result in the most impactful outcome. In the end, the student opted to graduate and enrolled in a program that was specifically designed to help them get into the field of work they wanted to be hired in. It was a scary leap for them, yet it was a plan that they were able to make. As an 18-year-old, this was the start of many big decisions they would need to make in their life, and the IEP process was able to model a way of critical thinking that will benefit them for years to come.

Another approach with strong benefits in the use of student strengths in our classrooms is that of peer tutoring. There are many models for peer tutoring with Same-age Peer Tutoring being the one we like best. In Same-age Peer Tutoring,

> [p]eers who are within one or two years of age are paired to review key concepts. Students may have similar ability levels or a more advanced student can be paired with a less advanced student. Students who have similar abilities should have an equal understanding of the content material and concepts. When pairing students with differing levels, the roles of tutor and tutee may be alternated, allowing the lower performing student to quiz the higher performing student. Answers should be provided to the student who is lower achieving when acting as a tutor in order to assist with any deficits in content knowledge. Same-age peer tutoring, like classwide peer tutoring, can be completed within the students' classroom or tutoring can be completed across differing classes. Procedures are more flexible than traditional classwide peer tutoring configurations.
> (Hott et al., 2012)

In this approach, we actively search for peers who are interested in taking an elective at middle or high school and receiving credit for their tutoring work. They are assigned a period to support a class or group of students. Tutors can be individuals with or without disabilities; all they need is the interest to be a tutor and an educator who can thoughtfully pair them in a class or group that they can assist. We then offer coursework, often virtual or before school, on a monthly basis to teach tutors about their roles. We teach them about confidentiality, differentiation strategies, communication and more.

What we find time and time again is that this experience is life-changing for the peer and the tutor. Those who are peers receiving the assistance are often students with disabilities with varying needs. I've observed students in Significant Support Needs (SSN) classes with tutors who are sitting with them and assisting with their communication devices in a reading class. Similarly, I've seen tutors assisting in physical education (PE), helping students with physical disabilities engage in regular PE classes in groups with same-aged students. We often have tutors in highly academic classes, frequently assigning eighth graders to sixth-grade classes where they work with individuals or small groups to differentiate the content.

The peers who are receiving the help are so much more receptive to a peer than an adult in almost every case. Recently, I was observing in an autistic support classroom when a student was having a big behavioral outburst. Multiple adults tried to engage the student to leave the classroom and reset behavior. The teacher stepped back and observed, ensuring all students in the room were safe. He quietly spoke to a classroom paraeducator/aide and asked them to get one of the peer tutors from the next room. The peer came in a few minutes later. They quietly sat down next to the student, who was now actively refusing and turning their back to the class. The tutor put out their hand and didn't say a word and just waited. After several seconds, the autistic student reached out their hand, stood up and walked out of the room with the tutor. They walked safely to a nearby room with the teacher following behind. The tutor then began an activity that they had clearly worked on many times, and the rest of the day went forward beautifully. In this experience, the tutor had spent a lot of time learning about the autistic student and engaging in many tasks with them. Something like this doesn't happen overnight, yet with time and learning and the development of authentic peer partnerships, this type of experience happens regularly in schools that have peer tutoring.

The tutors who are providing the assistance are often students who are curious about becoming educators or other fields of community service. Recently, I was sharing with a group of executives how peer tutoring can impact a school when our association (union) president spoke up. She shared that her daughter was a peer tutor and is now in college. To this day, her daughter will say that peer tutoring was one of the best experiences of her entire school career. Tutors learn so much in the process of helping others, and they get to explore experiences that help them in determining interests and careers. They learn how to work with diverse individuals and make a difference in their school community. They leave with just as much growth and learning, if not more, than those they tutor.

When you begin to see students as strengths in and of themselves, there are endless opportunities to collaborate and value their opinions. How can you include student voice in school survey information? How can you meet with and interview students when looking at improvement strategies? Where can students join traditionally adult-led committees or groups? This student voice and expertise should carry significant weight, but often, it is the one voice that is left out as we lead special education. What would be the difference in your system if you included students more in your processes, committees and responder processes?

Closing Activity

Valuing Student Strengths

What is one way you've included student strengths and voice in your current work? Tell your story of success.

List two students you have supported directly and brainstorm at least one strength or area of interest of each. What is one thing you can do to support these students' teams in utilizing this strength to increase access to learning?

What is one action step you can commit to in this area? What is your time line for following up?

Notes

1 Dalphonse, A., *Functions of Behavior in ABA: Complete Guide*, Last modified n.d., Accessed on July 30, 2023, https://masteraba.com/functions-of-behavior/
2 Scott, L., Teacher Self-Efficacy with Teaching Students to Lead IEP Meetings: A Correlation Study on Administrative Support. *I-Managers Journal on Educational Psychology* (2011–2012).

References

Baumer, N. (2021). "What Is Neurodiversity?" *Harvard Health Publishing*, 2021, November 23. Retrieved from www.health.harvard.edu/blog/what-is-neurodiversity-202111232645

Hott, B., Walker, J., & Sahni, J.(2012). Peer Tutoring. *Council for Learning Disabilities*. Retrieved from https://council-for-learning-disabilities.org/peer-tutoring-flexible-peer-mediated-strategy-that-involves-students-serving-as-academic-tutors/

8

Attracting and Retaining Quality Staff

As we began drafting this book, we started to notice a new and concerning trend in special education: staffing shortages. In 2022–23, we were unable to fill several special education teacher positions for the first time that either of us could remember. That continued to get worse as we watched existing staff take on more to compensate and then get burnt out. As we prepared for the 2023–24 school year, we saw more staff move positions or leave education and were faced with significant numbers of positions to hire and a dwindling pool of qualified candidates to consider.

According to data from the Bureau of Labor Statistics, more than 270,000 public school teachers and other related staff are anticipated to leave the education field each year from 2016–26.[1] In our own district, we see a turnover rate of about 10 percent of staff annually. These are not all educators leaving the field but a combination of staff who are leaving and staff who are changing positions. In our most intensive special education roles, we see 30 percent turnover every year, with that rate increasing. In our post covid reality, we now hear about this concern in every journal, every conference and in our daily work as we struggle to find teachers to fill roles. Not only do we not want teachers to leave, but we want to keep them in positions as long as possible because the continuity is good for kids.

DOI: 10.4324/9781003453826-8

In the summer of 2021, we hired 43 special education staff throughout our district, three of which were internal position changes. In the summer of 2022, we hired 55 special education staff with about 14 internal position changes and another 5 or so other positions that remained unfilled. In the summer of 2023, we were in the process of hiring 84 new special education staff, with 26 of those as internal position changes. The trend is concerning.

How can we even begin to address this increasing issue to ensure special education staff are in place for the services we have to provide students? In our current reality, we are seeing increased numbers of students on IEPs, reduced amounts of funding and increased need to put efforts into retention and recruitment. The situation feels impossible.

There are hundreds of articles and lots of research that you can review that points to recruitment and retention strategies. As this book is about redesigning special education, we will guide you to those resources if you are looking for the more traditional pathways for addressing this need. This chapter will be dedicated to thinking through how collaborative approaches might enhance and improve our efforts for recruitment and retention of quality staff. We strongly believe that the essence of our collaborative approach, shared in prior chapters, is what can make the crucial difference in attracting and retaining quality staff.

Attracting/Recruiting New Staff

Recruitment of new staff has previously been a linear effort best demonstrated through a flow chart of first then steps. We begin by identifying an open position, human resources posts the position and then our special education leaders spend most of our efforts on the hiring side of the process. We spent a lot of time crafting the right questions and look-fors for interview committees and sitting in on interviews to use a critical eye to select the very best candidate. We would spend significant effort in reference checks, always listening for any red flags and seeking that dreamy candidate who was going to be the quintessential special educator.

In the last few years, we started to see candidate folders with zero candidates. Our historical and linear process has come to a halt, as we have frequent scenarios with no candidates to interview. Now, if we are viewing this as a form of communication—it tells us that our historical efforts are not working in this current climate. We are doing the exact same things and getting vastly different results. After reading this book, what do you think we need to do next?

We needed to seek partners and listen to understand the issue. In 2022, we sat on several committees and groups that explored this issue, and we heard many ideas about how we could do things differently. Principals asked for some hard-to-fill position incentives. Our association representatives asked for some barriers to be removed for posting jobs earlier. Our special education leadership team asked to create a better process for finding alternatively licensed candidates. Our teachers asked for more support systems for staff who are hired. We were able to work diligently on each of these items after listening and understanding the issue, but something was still missing- collaboration.

As you know, we believe that the power is in the process of collaboration. As I sat back and assessed the situation and realized that this was the missing piece, I realized that we needed a process to make this more collaborative. I wrote a list of all open positions up on some chart paper and next to it identified who needed to be a partner in hiring. For the autism position at one school, I needed the principal, an autism specialist on my team, but I also needed a human resources (HR) recruitment partner, my office assistant who would help scope out candidates and some community members who could help solicit interest as well as interview candidates. I wasn't quite sure how we were going to do this or what process would get us there, but I was convinced that this was my map of collaborators who were going to be necessary.

The next morning, I bought each of my HR directors a card and some candy, thanking them for their heroic efforts so far this year. They really deserved the appreciation, as they were facing these hiring concerns systemwide and were in the process of reorganizing. Without stating it, I was also laying the groundwork for the appreciation for their work ahead, as I knew I was going to work more closely with them than ever before. I met with one of the directors and asked them who could help me with recruitment efforts and who could help with processing creative ideas. I walked across the office and found another director, and asked her if we could post some future jobs to create a pool of candidates we could start talking with before our usual posting timeline. She brought out a notepad and brainstormed some ideas, and within a few days, we had some general job openings posted.

Next, I reached out to each special education director and each principal with a job opening to let them know we were going to partner on their job. I asked for an update and how we could help remove barriers to get things moving along. Prior to this, principals posted their jobs, and we posted ours, and we didn't really communicate much until hires were processed. This was different. I wanted the message to be that we were in this together.

A few weeks later, the general positions closed, and we had about 20 interested candidates that I began reaching out to. I wanted to get to know them and what they were interested in. I wanted them to know that my district was the most welcoming and desirable so that we could hire them as soon as positions were available. I had several phone calls and answered lots of questions while guiding them to job postings that were a good match for their interests and skills. Before our jobs were even released, I was the concierge to our community to lay the groundwork for what was ahead.

When specific jobs were posted a few weeks later, one of the HR representatives asked if schools were reaching out to their communities. Great idea! This was another collaboration—let the community know we are hiring paraeducators or an autism program teacher and see how they can help. This became a part of our discussion with principals. Simultaneously, we started to ask our specialists and groups to share postings. Can our occupational therapists send the posting to their friends and university listservs? Can our BCBA group send posts to their Facebook groups? Our teams began to get invested in helping to find candidates. Principals, therapists and teachers would send me contacts to talk to and help them learn more about our incredible district and the job openings. Together, we made this personal—staff were not just coming to a new job; they were coming to a district that cared enough to personally answer questions and tell them that hiring was one of our most important priorities.

Every two weeks, I emailed principals and asked for an update. A few even asked if they were doing something wrong, as they noticed that this was a different interaction from prior years. My response was that they were doing everything right—we were just going to be better partners in this process, as we hoped for better results.

Throughout these months, I'm fairly sure I drove HR crazy as my mindset shifted from their work as a behind-the-scenes resource to viewing them as a critical collaborative partner. I needed them, and I wanted them to be just as invested in hiring great staff as I was. I called or emailed HR representatives daily, giving them updates on our progress and asking for their help through some of the more complex scenarios.

The truth is that we are only in the early stages of this hiring crisis, and my mind is spinning around various other ways we can even further improve this collaboration. I don't pretend that I have all the solutions here to present to you, but I am certain that this new framework of collaboration is going to begin to solve this for special education leaders. Although we are still in the process for this hiring season, we have 80 of the open positions in the process of hiring and only 4 that we are still looking to fill. Already, we have filled more jobs and have fewer jobs remaining unfilled than in the year before.

One of my own goals is to explore this topic even more, and I hope to use the protocol in Chapter 9 to bring people together this fall to see how we can further improve what has started to work this year. I am certain that there are more partnerships in our community and more brilliant ideas that my colleagues have in other districts and throughout our state licensing teams that we have yet to tap into. I want to spend some time bringing in our private provider groups and advocates to see what they can add to the expertise in this area. I want to hear from principals what worked this year and what we can still do to make this even better. What can we do with our university partners to create better pipelines for future special educators? What can we do with our students and our current schools to create pathways to excite students to become educators and return to their districts? By looking outside of our department and asking these kinds of questions, there are innumerable possibilities for us to work on in addressing what started out as an impossible situation.

BOX 8.1   Partnerships in Attracting Quality Staff

- Principals
- Current teachers and service providers
- Community groups and newsletters
- HR
- Parents
- Universities
- District specialists
- Who would you add?

Retaining Quality Staff

If we were to ask you why you still work in education, what is the first thing that comes to mind? When I think about what drives me in special education leadership, the very first thing that comes to mind is my professional relationships, primarily my team, followed by the feeling that I have some unique purpose within my agency. I am guessing you would say something similar, and our reasons are not too far from those highlighted in the data. People often tell us they are leaving education due to the lack of resources or support, stagnant salaries, work-life balance, increasing student behaviors or safety concerns and inadequate preparation or support. Equally important are the things that make educators want to stay, including the meaningful work we all do, our colleagues, community, opportunities for leadership and professional development.

Unpacking the reasons that educators stay and leave the field is paramount for designing initiatives to retain quality educators. How can we create a system where educators not only want to work in their jobs but are also committed and feel ownership in the work that they do? How can we set up a climate and system that compels special educators, even in their hardest years, to love their jobs and remain with our schools? As you might imagine, we believe that collaboration provides a critical and new role in solving this challenge.

Meaningful Work

Principals, teachers and district leaders often find meaning by seeing their successes and progress. We lose special educators when they feel that they cannot make a difference. We've seen some excellent special educators who were making incredible impacts leave the field because they could not see how their work was making a difference.

As district specialists, we keep track of a lot of data. We track how many teams make referrals to us, how much we support the team with the specific learner, what level of support the student needs initially and what level the student needs after our consultation. Developing these measures is paramount in that it provides us with the evidence to support that a difference is being made at the student level. Without this progress monitoring, we might get mired down in our daily crisis with teams, schools and families. Over time, we have added outcome measures to support our work. Some of these include tracking the percentage of students who make progress toward their goals, number of students with IEPs who have reduced maladaptive behaviors and number of students who have been staffed out of special education or increased time in general education. Knowing where you started with these metrics is key to evaluating progress, and collecting ongoing longitudinal data allows refinement. We get excited at the end of each year to share our data charts and summarize the work that we have done because it allows us to know without question that the work we did had meaning.

The further we get from the classroom, the further we sometimes feel from being truly connected to the kids and their learning, which is likely a driving force for our draw to education. It can be hard not to connect our worth as educators to the "direct" contact we make with students. The deeper we get into special education leadership, the more distance we can feel from that meaning. How do you know that the work you are leading is trickling down to impact students? And how does this connection to students contribute to or impede your staying in education over time?

Classroom teachers and service providers need the same sort of awareness and celebration of the impact of their work. One way we can help retain them is by helping them see their own meaning in their work. I've worked with many educators who keep progress data; they see their students' progress, and they have no question that they are doing great and impactful work. For special education leaders, it can be crucial to help educators collect and analyze this data. When someone is having a challenging year, I often ask them what is going well and how they know it. If they can point to the 15 students who made progress on every goal, they can breathe easier when we have one or two who are not. We also need to help educators meet and share their celebrations. We often set up small professional learning opportunities where we ask special educators to share their student data and talk about their successes. We also find poster sessions or bright spot learning to be helpful methods to have educators share the things that they are doing well. We've seen many principals give special educators a school award or recognition or record a video that highlights specialized work. All of these things both highlight and share the impacts that our special educators have in their school communities and give them the confidence they need to come back from day to day and year to year.

In addition to data, we are at an expanded vantage point as special ed leaders. I think we hold a unique responsibility to share and collaborate around the data and successes happening in our system. The sheer quantity of schools and students we interact with provides a unique opportunity for us to preview successful interventions, see what is working, see what doesn't and refine. In a way, we are collectors of meaning, walking into schools or classrooms, collecting and curating the best bits and then delivering that information to others. By making a commitment to share our observations, we can expedite initiatives that might best support learners. We can help special educators know that they are doing successful, meaningful work and also help them see that they are a part of a system that is doing successful, meaningful work.

Colleagues

On a scale of 1 to 10, how would you rate your relationship with your immediate team? Do you have someone you would call if you needed to discuss a complex problem? Someone who would be honest with you but encourage growth? Teammates that work as hard as you do? How do your answers to these questions contribute to attracting and retaining quality staff?

Over time, we have become more and more convinced that these initiatives of forming quality collegial relationships need to be formalized. Just as collaboration is key to special education leadership, it is key to the relationships that keep individuals in their jobs.

In our department, we believe we have a critical role in this work. As special education leaders, we create professional learning opportunities in small-group professional learning communities. We create new educator orientations and learning pathways that bring people together to build these relationships. We think about the multiple layers of support needed when someone needs help from someone outside of their school. We host small-group virtual late-start sessions to bring people together on content of their choice. By creating a network of colleagues, our special educators don't ever have to feel alone.

Principals play a key role in this work as well. Developing that climate at each school is necessary to retain staff. Too often, we see special education staff who don't feel a part of their school community, and as a result, we see high turnover in those schools. In the locations where we have teachers who know they hold a meaningful role in a school community, we see significantly less turnover in staff.

Create Community

My mom is an occupational therapist, and I have the pure pleasure of now leading a group of occupational and physical therapists in my district. When we hire new staff, we spend a year creating deep connections and learning communities with the new staff. This goes beyond the individual colleague relationships to include a community of care. When they are hired, the group liaison reaches out and meets with them personally. We assign secondary mentors and have everyone in the group participate in leading and learning during our group meetings. Everyone is lifted up as experts, and even the newest person in the group is asked to contribute as a leader. What has resulted is a community where these individuals want to host holiday celebrations and book studies at each other's homes. They throw parties when new babies are arriving and bring blankets and care packages when their colleagues have losses in their lives. It is a true community that is collectively thinking about and caring for each other. When we interview potential staff for open positions, we often hear that they are attracted to our district because they have heard about this community of care. We also have very little turnover, as individuals have a hard time finding any other group that would give them the personal and professional support that we do.

This creation of a community is one way that schools and departments can retain staff. Although deep and meaningful work is important, the connections, relationships and care must also be attended to for people to remain in their positions for the entirety of their careers.

In our unique vantage point, we see this as a point of failure all the time—schools that have leaders who focus only on the content and management aspect of their community see high levels of staff turnover. The administrators who can attend to the content and management but also host pancake breakfasts and book groups, provide thank you cards and care packages and truly set up a caring community tend to have very little turnover.

Opportunities for Leadership

Working in education is a long game, and staying invested and fresh can be a daunting task. Many of us know that we are committed to retiring from the education system, but the thought of doing our current job for the rest of our careers might be daunting. If you stay more than two years, you are probably familiar with initiatives that have been developed, implemented, unsuccessful, rebranded and then reintroduced as new. This cycle can be exhausting. Have you ever sat through a professional development that reminds you of content you have heard countless times, only using different terminology? We can tackle this exhaustion and repetition for some of our staff by finding opportunities for leadership.

One approach to leadership is encouraging and honoring the graduate coursework taken by special education staff. In our district, employees are compensated for any additional graduate schooling they engage in by being able to submit said credit to move up the salary scale. Local schools and agencies offer a variety of continuing education to teachers, and teachers quickly move up the pay scale. In addition to moving up the pay scale, this learning also increases their knowledge and application of the best practices in the field, thus helping them stay effective in the classroom. We can contribute to teacher retention if we have a firm understanding of each individual's professional goals, strengths, and preferences.

In our district, we have highly specialized intensive learning centers. Each center consists of learners with IEPs who have intensive needs. We have intensive learning centers for some of our students with autism, students with significant cognitive barriers and significant affective needs. This work is hard, and this role has the highest turnover rate of any of our special education roles. We have had to be intentional about what other roles might allow us to retain intensive teachers but might also allow them to move into other similar roles. For example, currently, half of our behavior analyst team were originally intensive teachers. It would have been easy to encourage them to stay or even leave for another district or role, but knowing their professional goals and supporting them through the process benefited everyone, as we were able to retain them in our district.

As we create professional learning plans for the year, we bring in a group of teacher leaders to help plan. We also bring in teacher leaders to run content sessions and small groups at every opportunity we can. This not only supports great content provided by those doing the work, but it also gives our teachers and providers opportunities to grow and develop their own interest in leadership. We don't want staff to have to leave us to find those opportunities, so we must create them.

Recently, we also reinvested in peer tutoring. This was another opportunity for leadership at our schools where staff could get additional pay for creating and leading a peer tutoring program. This peer tutoring opportunity helped our educators find incredibly meaningful work that they were passionate about; it offered them some additional pay and leadership opportunities. In its first year systematized in our district, all 15 of the staff who led the peer tutoring programs returned for a second year. Peer tutoring is one of our favorite leadership opportunities that has so many far-reaching benefits; however, other opportunities fit the same need. For some staff, it is joining a committee for work they are passionate about or taking a training that they can share with their colleagues. Encouraging and supporting these opportunities for leadership can impact the decisions of staff who might otherwise be interested in leaving your district to find the growth opportunities they desire.

Compensation

I hesitate to put this section in this chapter, as so often there is just not more money to offer compensation as an incentive for retaining staff. The truth is that many staff will remain if they are paid well and feel that this pay is commensurate with the work they are asked to do. It is worth thinking about creative ways that compensation might be able to be considered in the area of retention.

In our work, we have seen systems for leadership credit and educational credit that provide increases in compensation for these additional efforts. We have also provided stipends for paraeducator/aide staff who complete highly specialized coursework, such as registered behavior technician. With increasing behavioral needs and threats occurring in our school systems, stipends that incentivize training in this area have multiple benefits. We've also seen a real benefit in opportunities to compensate staff for their time—providing subs to free them up for urgent work or providing after-school pay. Another great offer is to provide compensation in the form of time by stepping in to cover classes. When we see someone who is really overwhelmed, they often cannot consider a sub because they have to spend time writing sub plans. But if we offer to come to step in for an hour or two to free them up for the task, it becomes more reasonable. We've done this with principals and district staff to help teachers have time for compiling data or collaborating with general ed teachers when they are in a real backlog.

Often, these small things show staff that we value their time as they go above and beyond their role. This aligns with our collaborative approach because often, this cannot be done in isolation. We encourage you to talk with your associations, district leaders and HR team to see what small opportunities for compensation might be realistic to consider. Also, we encourage collaboration with your educators to find time to listen and then explore what types of compensation could be meaningful to provide the kinds of relief needed to keep staff returning.

As we've said before, there is not a magic and quick solution here. To address this challenge using collaboration is hard work. In the spring and summer of 2023, we worked harder than ever to fill over 80 vacant special education positions. In the three states and three districts I have worked in, I have never seen such effort needed to fill the most basic special education positions. Efforts in retaining staff are just as important to limit the number of positions we have to fill from year to year. By using some of this book's core concepts of the six not-so-easy steps for collaborative change, finding unexpected partners and seeking powerful processes, we think we can begin to make a dent in this increasing area of need.

Closing Activity

Explore Your Own Efforts

Identify one or two collaborative partners who could help in your recruitment efforts.

How do the special educators who work under your leadership find meaning in their work? What opportunities could be provided to help them explore this further or celebrate their successes?

What colleagues are most important to your own work and why?

How would you describe the community for those you lead? What can you do to improve this even more so that staff can't imagine leaving their work?

What leadership opportunities do you provide as a special education leader? Can you think of someone who really needs to be brought into this work this year?

Identify several special education staff who work under your leadership. Can you identify specialties or passions they would like to grow? If not, how can you find out?

Note

1 Bureau of Labor Statistics, *Projections for Teacher: How Many Are Leaving the Occupation*, Last modified October 2018, Accessed on July 28, 2023, https://www.bls.gov/careeroutlook/2018/data-on-display/how-many-teachers-are-leaving.htm.

9

Designing Your Innovation

Now that you've had a chance to explore various ways to redesign special education through collaborative approaches, we want to take the opportunity to support you through a design process that is personalized to your current needs and work. We'd ask that you have a timer and a writing utensil before you read further. You can write responses directly in this book in the spaces provided or find a separate place to write down your responses.

Set aside a quiet time and space to work through the activities one by one to guide you to action steps for your personalized redesign plan. We ask that you give in to the process of creation and let the steps lead you to wherever they lead. The time limits are there to keep you thinking quickly rather than deeply at each step—do your best to stick to the time limits and stop when the timer goes off. You may be surprised with what comes out of the time. You also might find that working through this process now might result differently than it will in another year or two. Keep the book on hand and use this as a leadership tool that can help guide growth in times of renewal or help guide a path for resolution when many challenges are piled up at once. Remember, the power is in the process!

Activity 1

Brainstorm five current challenges or areas of conflict in your current role as a special education leader
Timer – 3 minutes

1.
2.
3.
4.
5.

Activity 2

Review your list above and circle only one that you'd be interested in exploring and innovating further.
Timer – 1 minute

Activity 3

Brainstorm as many creative solutions as possible to address the challenge you circled. Solutions can be realistic or unrealistic. If you get stuck with ideas, review our chapter headings to spark some thinking.
Timer – 5 minutes

Activity 4

Review your list for activity 3 and sort these into categories to see what themes arise. The grid below could help as an organizer, or you could use color coding, lists or any other quick format to define your categories.
Timer – 3 minutes

Activity 5

Identify three partners who should be brought in to join this brainstorm with you, one of which must be someone outside of the school setting.
Timer – 2 minutes

1.
2.
3.

Activity 6

Create a plan to involve your partners and begin to investigate possible solutions.
Timer – no timer. Action occurs over several days or weeks.

- How will I reach out to the three partners in activity five to invite them to brainstorm these ideas?

- When can we meet?

- How will I frame the need and reason to brainstorm together? Write down how you will define the problem to solve and why you need their input.

- Create an agenda for your discussion. Will you work together to investigate ideas you've brainstormed or do that after you meet? Will you collectively plan to discuss action steps or keep this time together only for input?

Activity 7

Once you've completed activity 6, make a list of any research that is needed to investigate any of the brainstormed items to determine viability. Then take the time to investigate each item.
Timer – no timer. Action occurs over several days or weeks.

-
-
-
-
-

Activity 8

Now it's time to refine your brainstorms and determine some next steps. Answer the questions below to guide the creation of action steps.

Timer – 10 minutes

- ♦ After researching ideas from the brainstorm and hearing from partners, the following represents real and actionable ideas that we will explore.

- ♦ What is the role of partnerships and collaboration in designing an action plan for these ideas? Why will partners and collaboration improve this process?

♦ Remind yourself of the original challenge to remain focused. What is the problem that we are trying to solve?

♦ Identify the first three to five actions to take to actualize the real and actionable steps identified here in activity 8. Write them down and use this as your road map to begin.

For Product Safety Concerns and Information please contact our EU
representative GPSR@taylorandfrancis.com
Taylor & Francis Verlag GmbH, Kaufingerstraße 24, 80331 München, Germany

www.ingramcontent.com/pod-product-compliance
Lightning Source LLC
Chambersburg PA
CBHW050557300426
44112CB00013B/1967